Figures in a Red Landscape

Pilar Bonet

Figures in a
Red Landscape

Translated from the Spanish
by
Norman Thomas di Giovanni
and
Susan Ashe

The Woodrow Wilson Center Press
Washington, D.C.

The Johns Hopkins University Press
Baltimore and London

Editorial Offices
The Woodrow Wilson Center Press
370 L'Enfant Promenade, S.W.
Suite 704
Washington, D.C. 20024-2518 U.S.A.

Order from:
The Johns Hopkins University Press
Hampden Station
Baltimore, Maryland 21211
Telephone 1-800-537-5487

Printed in the United States of America
∞ Printed on acid-free paper

9 8 7 6 5 4 3 2 1

Library of Congress Cataloging-in-Publication Data

Bonet, Pilar.
    [Imágenes sobre fondo rojo.   English]
    Figures in a red landscape / Pilar Bonet ; translated from the
Spanish by Norman Thomas di Giovanni and Susan Ashe.
        p.   cm.
    Includes index.
    ISBN 0-943875-45-5 (alk. paper)
    1. Soviet Union—History—1985-1991.   I. Title.
DK286.B6613   1993   93-16722
947.085'4—dc20   CIP

WOODROW WILSON INTERNATIONAL CENTER FOR SCHOLARS

The Center is the "living memorial" of the United States of America to the nation's twenty-eighth president, Woodrow Wilson. The U.S. Congress established the Woodrow Wilson Center in 1968 as an international institute for advanced study, "symbolizing and strengthening the fruitful relationship between the world of learning and the world of public affairs." The Center opened in 1970 under its own presidentially appointed board of directors.

In all its activities the Woodrow Wilson Center is a nonprofit, nonpartisan organization, supported financially by annual appropriations from the U.S. Congress, and by the contributions of foundations, corporations, and individuals.

WOODROW WILSON CENTER PRESS

The Woodrow Wilson Center Press publishes the best work emanating from the Center's programs and from Fellows and Guest Scholars, and assists in publication, in-house or outside, of research works produced at the Center and judged worthy of dissemination. Conclusions or opinions expressed in Center publications and programs are those of the authors and speakers and do not necessarily reflect the views of the Center staff, fellows, trustees, advisory groups, or any individuals or organizations that provide financial support to the Center.

For my father, Antonio Bonet

Contents

───────■───────

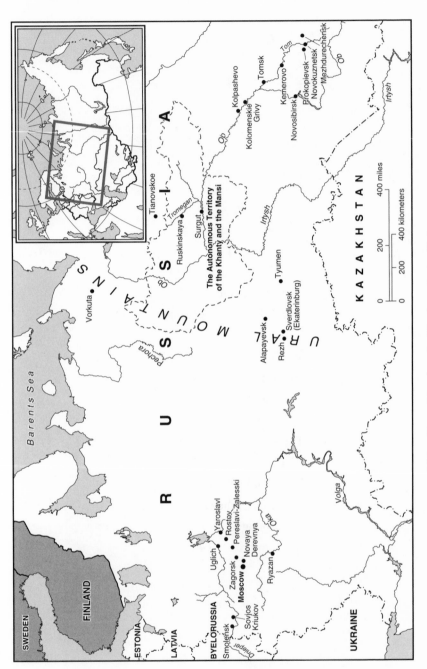

Major Places Mentioned—Northern Soviet Union

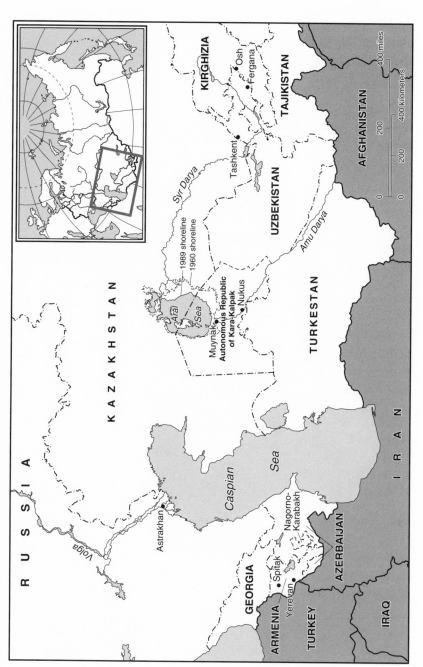

Major Places Mentioned—Southern Soviet Union

Introduction

———————■———————

THIS book was conceived as a collection of sketches, drawn from unusual angles—landscapes and portraits, both group and individual—that would depict day-to-day human drama in the then Soviet Union during its transition from an ideology-ridden, totalitarian system that was simultaneously repressive and protective toward an unregimented society characterized by freedom and insecurity.

I arrived in the Soviet Union as a correspondent for *El País*, the Madrid daily, in January 1984. It was the eve of the great changes that were beginning to stir that stagnant land. Then, in March 1985, Mikhail Gorbachev came to the fore and initiated a process of reform that the world came to know as perestroika. For the next seven years I was to report on unfolding events.

Perestroika was a brief stage, a bridge between two very different eras. I began this book when disillusionment was replacing hope as the general state of mind. It was the summer of 1990. The Soviet Union had reached the limit of its capacity for reform, and perestroika was nearing its last gasp. The man in the street could no longer be persuaded that the Communists, headed by President Gorbachev, were capable of the radical change that the country required.

The West, however, anxious to continue believing in Gorbachev's statements from the Kremlin, did not give sufficient credence to this state of mind. The West did not hear the voices that spoke in frustration and discontent from the remotest corners of the country. Today those ephemeral voices help us understand why Gorbachev's program of limited reforms from above was doomed to failure.

This book is a kind of family album, but one with a difference. It makes no attempt to include snapshots of all the relatives or of the prominent ones, whose faces are already in the limelight. Instead, it tries to portray a few of the lesser-known family members and, in particular, some of the country cousins.

Life in the provinces was different from life in Moscow. Out in the hinterlands Western observers were continually finding that they had to correct opinions they had formed in the capital of a country too big to be understood from a single vantage point. I had a hunch that the provinces might prove a breeding ground for new phenomena and that they would revive and refresh the political life of the Soviet Union. Today's Russian leadership, most of it originating from outside Moscow, confirms my hunch, although not quite in the way I had envisaged.

Until recently, Western correspondents in the capital were restricted in their access to the interior. Most of the Soviet land mass was simply out of bounds. This situation is slowly changing but remains problematic. Some of the places I visited while writing this book—the Siberian city of Tomsk, say, or Rezh, in the Urals—were closed to foreigners until the beginning of the 1990s.

My choice of the people included here was governed in large part by chance. I was sure that anyone I came across in my travels was undergoing the same crisis of values and identity that affected the rest of the Soviet Union. Each person I spoke to showed a particular blend of the doubt and insecurity generated by a breakdown in norms of behavior and an absence of new guidelines. I was keen to explore the changes and traumas that individuals were experiencing. Above all, I wanted to get inside people's heads. I decided to avoid Muscovite politicians and intellectuals, who knew little about their own country, and public figures, who were used to handling the press. To protect identities, only in one chapter—the one on Armenia—did I feel it necessary to give any of the characters different names.

Introduction

One almost tangible impression that I had in the summer of 1990 was of a people no longer operating from a collective sense of "sovietness" but beginning to find new identities in reemerging national cultures. For many, Russia and Boris Yeltsin became a focus for what remained of the illusions unsatisfied by perestroika and Gorbachev. It grew increasingly clear that the economic, political, and ideological changes my characters were embroiled in were taking place against the background of a dying empire. People who thought they were citizens of a feared, all-powerful state now found themselves caught up in its death throes, much like the victims of an earthquake or shipwreck.

As I traveled in Aeroflot's crowded, uncomfortable planes, my word processor at the ready, the investigation I had set out on began to take over and color my mind. The reality I encountered was much more primitive and complex than anything I had imagined. The provinces were there before my very eyes in all their crudeness and tedium. Some of the hidden charm I thought I had unearthed evaporated in platitudes.

Throughout my journeys there were wonderful moments, unforgettable excursions through unique landscapes, and generous, hospitable people. Even so, my recollections are tinged by sadness at the general lack of prospects and at the appalling environment, which weighed like a millstone on all those who were trapped there.

The assassination in 1990 of Father Aleksandr Men, a Russian Orthodox priest of Jewish origin, affected me deeply. He had seemed a ray of hope, a breath of fresh air and reason in a floundering, prejudice-ridden society. His killer has not yet been found and the motive for the crime remains a mystery, but I am unable to dissociate his death from the anti-Semitism I witnessed on so many occasions in Russia. This connection convinced me to combine in a single chapter my experiences of anti-Semitism and my talks with Father Men, which took place the week he died and were the last interviews he ever gave.

My relationship with the characters in this book varied and evolved over time, and I make no attempt to judge them. I have the impression that each of them encapsulates a number of historical layers that do not always produce a harmonious blend, that they are actors in events that overwhelm them. Perhaps not all will manage to come to grips with the challenge that history has laid at their feet or free themselves from the mythic worldview that makes them believe in the destructive power of hidden forces. New generations will be needed, for today's adults belong to an incoherent universe and cannot readily find their place in a changing world.

When the coup of August 1991 was thwarted, the sense of a gradual evolution in Soviet life was superseded by a sense that there was now a radical break between past and present. It was as if time had split into before and after the coup, just as in 1917 it split into before and after the October revolution. But such breaks can be deceptive, for the past still intrudes forcibly on the present of the men and women who were once citizens of the Soviet Union.

Rupture and continuity are today woven together in a brand-new context. My characters, different as they are, join hands. They share anxieties, fears, and thoughts about the outside world. Listening to them reveal these anxieties and fears as they were living them has been a great privilege.

After the failed coup, in which a group of high-ranking Soviet officials tried to put the brakes on history, I re-visited some of my characters in their homes. The outcome of our meetings is contained in the epilogue of this book. No longer part of an amorphous mass, these men and women were asserting their identities as distinctive figures in a reality that was growing ever harsher. For the first time in their lives, they were freely exploring their unique, individual destinies.

A large part of this book was drafted and finished at the Kennan Institute for Advanced Russian Studies in Washington, D.C., where I spent the nine months from November 1991 through July of the following year as a research scholar. I should like to thank Blair Ruble, the institute's director, for having provided me with the peace and intellectual stimulation in which I was at last able to give these pages their final shape.

Pilar Bonet
Ibiza, Spain
1 September 1992

Figures in a Red Landscape

1

■

Salt

Desert and steppe cover most of the Central Asian Autonomous Republic of Kara-Kalpak, whose area of some sixty-three thousand square miles and population of around 1,300,000 are an administrative part of Uzbekistan. The Kara-Kalpak region has become a victim of over-ambitious engineering projects begun in the Leonid Brezhnev era. Siphoned off for irrigation purposes, the sixteen hundred–mile Amu Darya, the ancient Oxus, can no longer be counted on to replenish the Aral Sea, into which it empties. During the past twenty-five years, the dying Aral has shrunk to two-thirds of its former size. The Kara-Kalpak people are descended from seminomadic Turkic tribes that were incorporated into the Russian Empire in 1873. Soviet education did not succeed in wiping out either the republic's Islamic traditions or its tribal differences. Nukus, the capital, located on the vast delta of the Amu Darya, is a decaying city of 175,000 inhabitants.

IN the heartland of Central Asia a new desert is in birth. A fine sand that leaves a salty film on one's face advances stealthily but implacably over the shrinking waters of the Aral Sea and is carried far beyond it by the wind.

The Aral, once the world's fourth-largest inland sea, is still described in encyclopedias and geography books as a body of water located between the Soviet republics of Kazakhstan and Uzbekistan, the southern part of the sea falling within the Autonomous Republic of Kara-Kalpak. Two of Asia's great rivers, the Amu Darya and the Syr Darya, flow into it.

The geography books are out of date. So much of the Aral

1

has dried up that the sea has split in half. Soviet astronauts had been warning of this event for some time. Ecologists now calculate that the large-scale shrinkage of the Aral Sea is the first step in a major disaster that will turn Central Asia into a desert. As if this weren't enough, the region suffers from a dearth of industrial development and a population explosion.

The cracked, arid soil that the Aral Sea has yielded up and that is now in the process of colonization by desert fauna and micro-organisms stands as damning evidence of Soviet policy throughout Central Asia during the 1960s and 1970s. The Aral is the victim of a misguided centralized plan whereby vegetable gardens and orchards, carefully tended for hundreds of years, were sacrificed to single-crop cultures of rice or cotton. The policy, whose creators gave little thought to the consequences, called for the irrigation of thousands upon thousands of acres, while to boost productivity it made unstinting use of chemical fertilizers, pesticides, and defoliants. By the perverse logic of the scheme, rivers were diverted from their courses to the Aral, and toxic waste was fed back into its waters. By the same logic the fields were flooded, causing salt to be dredged up from the bowels of the earth.

The Autonomous Republic of Kara-Kalpak, one of the Soviet Union's poorest domains, is probably the region that will most suffer from the drying up of the Aral Sea. Kara-Kalpak is already suffering. It endures a record-breaking infant mortality, its children are prey to rickets and vitamin deficiencies, and its young men no longer grow tall enough for military service. Kara-Kalpak's women are weakened by various types of anemia that lower their resistance to disease. This affliction leaves them without the strength to battle their way out of Islam's cultural labyrinths—arranged marriages, for example. With glasnost, the Soviet press has been full of stories of Central Asian women who, rather than contract such marriages, have committed suicide by setting fire to themselves.

Since the sand is swallowing up their world, the very identity of the men and women of Kara-Kalpak is bound up in the death throes of the Aral Sea. Once fishermen, the Kara-Kalpaks still keep angling rods in their back rooms and, hidden away in a cupboard, a can or two of tasty Aral Sea fish. Today these cans, without "use by" dates, seem relics of a bygone world. The Kara-Kalpaks are fond of recalling—not without a trace of bitterness—that in the 1920s Vladimir Lenin asked the Aral fishermen for help in wiping out hunger along the Volga.

The Kara-Kalpaks are captains of cargo ships that no longer sail and officials in charge of ports that no longer exist. They are men and women whose daily affairs are still tied to the slow rhythms of the past. Appearing to live in a mirage, they gaze up at the sky or at the Amu Darya or toward the distant rivers of Siberia, waiting for a miracle that will bring water. They take one look at the blazing midday sun and bury themselves until evening in the dimness of their homes, almost as if they were turning into a new species of desert animal.

Nukus, the capital of Kara-Kalpak, is a remote city. Its remoteness, however, lies not in the physical distance that separates it from other cities but in its essence, which is beyond tangible objects or space. Nukus is remote because its inhabitants are marooned in an unreal world, a place that has ceased in part to exist. Nobody comes here for pleasure. Until 1989, the city was off limits to foreigners. There was no strategic reason for this; there was only the poverty and shame. No tourists visit Nukus, not even Soviet tourists. It figures in none of the state travel agency Intourist's arduous itineraries through the interior of the USSR.

By day, the temperature rises above one hundred degrees, and the salt that carpets the ground shines so brightly that it dazzles the eye. The gardens of Nukus are a vanguard of the desert. By night, the frogs croak in the stagnant irrigation ditches, and from the apartment houses, which are little more than barracks, the sweating, dehydrated inhabitants come out for a breath of fresh air. Nukus nights are full of phantoms that hide by day.

In this world of phantoms lives Gulaita Esmuratova, wife of the academician Kalibek Kamalov. She painstakingly embroiders the face of the poet Aleksandr Pushkin in cross-stitch while deploring the bigamous practices of some of the community's most respected men. Gulaita belongs to a generation of Asiatic women for whom Soviet communism was a liberating force. Her Communist militancy and her past as an heiress to a wealthy, noble Muslim family have made for an unusual blend. Esmuratova fought for the abolition of the *kalim,* the dowry that is still paid for Central Asian brides. Gulaita is an author. She writes about the women of Kara-Kalpak as she sits amid pictures of the Virgin and Child and a naked Venus. "Sure, you're free, you Western women," she says. "I envy you. The things you do are not possible here."

Also living among phantoms is a former local museum curator, a pensioner who could not marry the woman he loved because he did not have enough money to pay the *kalim.* Another resident, Orazbai Abdirakhmanov's wife, has not escaped the phantoms, either. A friend hanged herself because the man with whom she had just entered into a marriage contract did not make her happy. The daily life of Nukus is woven of such phantoms.

I first met the writer Orazbai Abdirakhmanov in Moscow in the autumn of 1988 at a conference about the Aral Sea. It was the beginning of a friendship that was to continue in Nukus and in Tashkent. Orazbai had taken part in an expedition organized by the Soviet Writers' Union, which had visited all those Asiatic territories affected by the ecological disaster.

Orazbai first realized that the situation was grave, possibly irreversible, when his elderly mother began refusing the cups of black tea that she drank every day. Orazbai's mother, who was dying of cancer, complained that the tea was salty. She died in December 1981. It was a year of great hardship, when even the cows belonging to the neighboring sovkhozy and kolkhozy—the two types of Soviet farms, state and collective—would not drink the well water. Saturated with chemicals, the Amu Darya flowed past Nukus on its way to the Aral Sea. Part of its waters remained upstream in the artificial lakes and on the fields that the Amu Darya ran through before reaching Kara-Kalpak. Today water is still a bone of contention among the people who live along the banks of Asiatic rivers. Where water is concerned there is no solidarity among Uzbeks, Turkmen, and Kara-Kalpaks. Those living closest to the mouth of a river have to put up with whatever is disposed of by the people nearest its source.

Eventually, Orazbai's children also refused to drink their morning tea. They too found the water salty, and all day they went about with dry mouths, looking for some liquid to quench their thirst. The calamity had been building up gradually, but Orazbai only became aware of it when his mother would not drink her tea. Orazbai had long since given up angling, which had been one of his favorite pastimes. By now, no one could fish in the Aral Sea, where Orazbai and his family used to go every summer. They flew on a small plane from Nukus to Muynak and then made the rest of the journey overland along the coast by car. Orazbai never imagined that the disaster would touch him personally or affect his life the way it has.

Every year in Muynak the residents repaint the sign welcoming visitors to the Aral Sea, but every day the town itself is growing farther and farther away from the water's edge.

"We are a salted people, a people pickled in brine," says Orazbai, eagerly gulping the mineral water brought by his foreign visitor. "I'm always thirsty, always parched."

Orazbai has never before seen a bottle of Western mineral water like the liter and a half I bought in a Moscow hard-currency shop. "Does this stuff last?" he asks, tapping the plastic container with a finger.

Orazbai is a descendant of the White Horde, one of the branches of Mongols who first populated these steppes, and he is a patriotic Kara-Kalpak. In the name of his country, he has fought to keep alive a sea that he now looks on sorrowfully, without hope.

Orazbai has founded the Kara-Kalpak Society, whose aim is to rescue the Aral Sea. The group has been registered and has a bank account. He is its president, but its struggle has fallen into skepticism and nostalgia. Soon, when the authorities—who still bar the shores of the Aral Sea to travelers without a special permit—finally decide to allow groups of Western visitors in, they will be able to choose from among several desert routes. Some of these may run in concentric circles, tracing the coastline of the Aral Sea down through the decades.

Whenever he visits Tashkent, the capital of Uzbekistan, Orazbai rushes to the nearest faucet and gulps down the running water, which is not especially renowned for its quality. To Orazbai, used to the salt of Kara-Kalpak, a dirty washbasin in a Tashkent hotel seems like a fountain and the faucet a jet of crystal-clear water.

Besides being a writer, Orazbai is director of the Kara-Kalpak Film Studios, a somewhat pompous name for a building which even before it is finished has begun to show signs of decay. The walls are flaking, and the seats in the projection room are coming apart at the seams. This state of affairs is fairly common in the Soviet Union wherever an area is trying to establish its cultural autonomy on a tiny budget. Orazbai's studios are caught up in the same atmosphere of unreality that envelops everyone in Kara-Kalpak. Against all the odds, the studios affirm a will to live.

Orazbai makes the long journey to Tashkent fairly frequently but not simply because Kara-Kalpak has, since 1936, been an autonomous republic under the jurisdiction of Uzbekistan. He goes to develop the films that he shoots in his studios. Kara-Kalpak's salty water would ruin them.

As the voice of protest for a society that is otherwise asleep, Orazbai makes documentaries denouncing the Aral Sea's ecological degradation, recording for posterity the stories of erstwhile skippers who have had to exchange the sea for a fish tank in the backyard. He shoots the ramshackle interior of a mansion that once stood on the seafront. Originally built for the leisure use of Communist party officials from neighboring Uzbekistan, it stands today in the middle of a desert like some abandoned temple.

Olympus is no more. Its gods have disappeared. Among them

was Sharaf Rashidov, the top party bigwig of Uzbekistan, related by marriage to Kalibek Kamalov, the top party bigwig of Kara-Kalpak. Rashidov, who wanted to be remembered as an Asiatic Maecenas, died in a car crash in 1983. Kamalov was arrested in 1986 on a charge of taking bribes. These were the men who made gifts to Brezhnev of Central Asia's all-time bumper cotton crops and in whom the Soviet leadership placed their trust. In his camp Rashidov had the Soviet Union's Ministry of Water and other institutions that spent all their time digging waterways in order to fulfill plans that rewarded those who shifted the most soil.

Today all those institutions have made an about-face and placed themselves at the service of the effort to save the Aral Sea. Orazbai likens them to a gang of killers trying to resuscitate their victim. By now nobody thinks the Aral Sea can be revived. All anyone can do is prevent it from drying up completely and leaving behind the very fine dust that will condemn the seabed to becoming a desert. It no longer matters whether the water flowing into the sea is clean or dirty so long as it covers the deadly sand.

Kara-Kalpak, the land of skippers without ships and ships without a sea, is in the throes of a painful death. What happens to such a region when its specialty is sturgeon? What happens when its way of life is sustained by fishing?

In a glass case in the Nukus museum are tins of fish from the Muynak cannery. These few cans, if placed on the shelves of a supermarket, would be bought in all innocence by any Soviet consumer. They are all that remain of the fish that once swam in the Aral Sea.

The fish have disappeared, but—a sign of just how out of touch with reality Soviet planning is—the Muynak cannery still operates, supplied with fish that comes in refrigerated freight cars all the way from the Pacific coast. In this way, about a thousand people give some meaning to their existence and perpetuate the illusion of living in a city of fishermen. Statistics show that in 1989 the production of canned fish actually rose.

On the overheated sands that the sea has left behind in its inexorable retreat lie the hulks of the fishing boats that once made up the Aral fleet. They were used for both fishing and shipping. Orazbai would have liked these hulks to remain stranded there forever, like beached whales, but his wish was not granted. Steel is scarce, and the cooperatives cut up the hulls with acetylene torches. The cooperatives make good use of the scrap metal, which has a price. To Orazbai the disaster is beyond any price.

Orazbai divides the life of the Aral Sea into two periods: before and after the creation of the Soviet Ministry of Irrigation and Water, in 1966. This body justified its existence by carrying out gigantic canal and irrigation projects that employed millions of people. According to the rationale of the system there was a direct relation between the scale of an undertaking and its success. The greater the amount of water and pesticides used, the more satisfactory the project. The ministry had its plan, which in turn was linked to the plan for cultivating cotton and rice. To increase the acreage under cultivation and improve soil fertility, dams and more dams were built. All the kolkhozy and sovkhozy that grew cotton and rice wanted their own small sea, their own pond. Each stole water that would otherwise have flowed from the Amu Darya into the Aral Sea.

When the Aral's waters began to recede dramatically, the central institutions reassured the inhabitants of the region. What did they want the Aral for, anyway? What did it matter if the sea disappeared? The Soviet state would turn it into a cotton field. What the people had to do was complete the irrigation system. More than one high-ranking official spoke out in favor of the disappearance of the sea, which stood in the way of plans for the large-scale cultivation of cotton and rice.

Orazbai now knows that life goes on in the desert, too. Otherwise where do those rats that carry the plague come from? These are the creatures that a special institute set up in Nukus will exterminate before the city is infested.

In his latest documentary, Orazbai filmed the ravaged, disfigured faces of the lepers from the Kran-tau colony, near Nukus. The thousand or so sufferers confined in this lazaretto, he believes, are a symbol of Kara-Kalpak. "The lepers," Orazbai claims, "are cut off from society." Among the Kran-tau patients is a ship's captain who once sailed the waters of the Aral Sea. Kara-Kalpak is full of such captains without vessels, especially in Muynak, the erstwhile fishermen's haven that now lies a good fifty miles from the seashore. Orazbai maintains that in summer the coastline shrinks by nearly one-eighth of an inch an hour, and it is by inches of desert that he measures his thoughts, his words, and the passage of time.

Orazbai has never laid eyes on a credit card, and he thinks that the Swedes, who have offered him a few thousand rubles to act as adviser on a film about the Aral Sea, are paying him an astronomical sum. The subject is ideal for an ecological film, especially one aimed at a developed, philanthropic society. Orazbai has no idea what the money can buy. He has no points of reference beyond the reality of Kara-Kalpak, where he takes his bearings from nature. The world, he believes, is as good, as hospitable, and as generous as he is.

Nukus, July 1989, and Tashkent, August 1990

2

———————— ■ ————————

The Garden

The Central Asian Republic of Uzbekistan, with an area of about 172,000 square miles, has a population of over twenty million, of whom some 70 percent are Uzbeks and the rest mainly Russians (8.3 percent), Tadzhiks (4.7 percent), and Kazakhs (4.1 percent). Alarmed by ethnic tensions in recent years, many Russian residents have fled the republic. Tashkent, the capital, is a populous ancient city with more than two million inhabitants. Its name first appears in Chinese dynastic chronicles in the second century B.C. Located on the age-old trade route from Samarkand to Beijing, Tashkent came under Arab and later Seljuk rule. In the thirteenth and fourteenth centuries, the city was taken, respectively, by Genghis Khan and Tamerlane. Despite serious damage from the earthquake of 1966, Tashkent still has a large number of buildings of historic or artistic interest. Tashkent became part of the Russian Empire in 1865 and by 1899 was linked by rail to Russia and Europe.

O LD Petya had just sat down under the grape arbor and begun to eat when his son Volodya burst into the garden. The dog started to bark. Turning aside from the table and his bowl of soup, Petya put on his shirt. He had taken it off the better to manage the jobs that Volodya had given him.

For the first time in his life, Petya would have central heating and a bathroom. Before setting off for Moscow, Volodya wanted to see his father comfortable in the house that had been the younger man's first home. He also wanted the house, where Petya had been living alone since the death of his wife and elder son, to be a base for him in Tashkent, a place to which Volodya could always come home. To this end, he had kept a room of his own with a view of the garden, hoping one day to put a word processor in it. Volodya's fondest dream was to be able to have such a machine in the house where he had once spent so much time working at his schoolbooks.

Old Petya took a melon from the larder, then went down into the cellar for two bottles of his best wine. He had been making wine for thirty years from grapes picked on this same plot of land. Today was special, because Volodya—who was always so busy—had dropped in on him. Petya wanted to celebrate.

"One day they'll make mincemeat of you and spread your guts up and down the valley to teach the rest of us a lesson. Why do you keep getting into hot water? The way you don't seem to know how to behave toward those with more power than you, no one would ever imagine you grew up here in Central Asia."

Old Petya shooed away the flies that were buzzing around his plate, poured out the pink, sweetish wine, and grasped his spoon. He complained that the country was no longer being ruled with a firm hand, as it had been in Joseph Stalin's day. Petya was torn between pride in his son's achievements and an uncompromising view of the world in which there would be no place for Volodya.

"No one would ever imagine you could be so tactless," chimed in Aunt Valentina, who had come into the garden as soon as she heard Volodya's voice. Aunt Valentina lived next door. All the neighbors along the street were related to Volodya. They had divided up among them the big garden the grandfather had managed to withhold from collectivization, and on their individual plots they had built simple, one-story houses. These were somewhat inconvenient, without either running water or sewerage, but their owners were happy. They were centrally located and they had fruit trees, chicken coops, rabbits, and even a pond with beaver, which they sold to hatmakers. The situation was a lot better than being crammed together and having to put up with the heat in one of the modern apartment blocks that were exactly the same in Tashkent as in Moscow.

This was a pleasant neighborhood. Close by was a fruit and

vegetable market, where as a boy Volodya used to sell carnations and tomatoes. The garden had supplemented the family income, which consisted only of Petya's small wage as a telegraph operator and that of his wife, who had been a bookkeeper. Volodya had been good at selling. He was so friendly and polite that no one could resist him.

"If it weren't for the garden!" Aunt Valentina exclaimed as she drank a glass of her brother's old wine. Ever since Petya had been on his own, Valentina often came around to keep him company. She explained how Volodya learned to read at the age of five without having been taught. Aunts tell the same tales the world over. But Volodya began to squirm and seemed to be transformed, mustache and all, into a reincarnation of his childhood self. So much praise got on his nerves.

The man who here was plain Volodya—"our Volodya"—was known to the world as Soviet army Major Vladimir Zolotukhin, deputy to the Soviet Congress, member of the parliamentary Youth Commission, and Uzbekistan correspondent of the biweekly magazine *Sovetsky voin* (The Soviet Soldier). At the age of thirty-one, Zolotukhin was one of many democratically inclined military deputies and a member of the congressional Interregional Group.

The Zolotukhins were Russians. Their ancestors had come to Uzbekistan from Astrakhan, at the mouth of the Volga. They were peasants who at the end of the last century had bought land in the tsar's Asiatic dominions. They had learned to speak Uzbek, they cultivated the land like Uzbeks, and they withstood the torrid summer heat like Uzbeks. What more did it take to consider a country your own, wondered old Petya.

Until the Fergana valley killings of 3 and 4 June 1989, the Zolotukhins had never stopped to think about their ethnic origin. They took their existence in Uzbekistan for granted. The incident at Fergana changed all that. In this fertile but overpopulated valley, Uzbeks had slaughtered a hundred Turks, who had been their neighbors for decades, and then plundered and burned their houses. These Turks had been deported by Stalin in 1944 from Mtskhet, in Georgia, where they had lived for centuries as an ethnic minority. A squabble in a market had sparked the massacre. The army had been put on alert, but this did not prevent more killings the following year in Osh, farther up the Fergana valley, in the Kirghiz Republic. This time minority Uzbeks died at the hands of the Kirghiz.

The killings were brutal, appalling in their savagery. Major Zolotukhin had investigated the facts and sent videos back to Moscow showing burned and mutilated corpses. What led to such ritualistic cruelty, such mass ferocity? Years of suffering and oppression had all at once come to a head in an act of uncontrollable resentment against outsiders.

After the Fergana massacre, the Russians in Uzbekistan began to live in fear. The most apprehensive packed up their belongings and joined the swelling ranks of people in flight from ethnic unrest all over the Soviet Union. The exodus affected the Tashkent airplane factory, leading to a shortage of skilled technicians and jeopardizing development of the plant's next model. The factory might even have to consider moving to another republic, one where the people were not so tied to rural life or so dependent on the land for feeding their families, which by Uzbek tradition were large.

The Zolotukhins never once considered leaving. They did not see themselves as colonists, nor was their concept of a homeland a militant one. "My homeland is my house, my father, my wife, and my children," Zolotukhin maintained. The choice between Russia and Uzbekistan had been a hard one for Volodya. Both republics, both cultures, were harmoniously woven into his character. Inside his head, Zolotukhin kept intact a world that was falling apart all around him.

His mother tongue was Russian, but in the Russian heartland a pragmatist like Zolotukhin would have been unusual. His sense of hospitality, his respect for the family, the ritualistic way he sliced the melon, and the pleasure he took in savoring the fruit— all these were Uzbek. Added to these qualities were Zolotukhin's personal characteristics of curiosity and open-mindedness.

According to Aunt Valentina, Volodya had wanted to be a

soldier since he was a small boy. He was the first Zolotukhin to show a military bent and the first to receive higher education. The Tashkent Military Academy, however, had not readily admitted him. He had had to wait a year, during which time he learned to repair radios and teletype machines. The medal he was awarded for finishing his studies was the first golden object ever to enter old Petya's house.

Imperialism was the last thing on Zolotukhin's mind. He regarded the Soviet withdrawal from Eastern Europe as "a piece of common sense," because "it isn't ours." What worried him were practical matters, such as the lack of housing for returning soldiers. As soon as Zolotukhin left the dingy apartment in Tashkent where he lived with his wife and three children, it would be taken over by a fellow officer currently stationed in East Germany. The new tenant could consider himself lucky to have a roof over his head.

Disarmament and a reduction in the armed forces were not an altruistic gesture by Soviet policy makers. The cuts were a necessity, because the country could no longer afford such a large army. In Zolotukhin's words, it was "a step away from madness toward a more natural state." Besides, young men—wanting to serve in their home republics—were more and more determined to resist conscription into the Soviet army.

Zolotukhin favored a gradual shift to a professional army, with alternative service for conscientious objectors. However, he still had not said what he thought a new Soviet army should be like. Nor had he replied to a more basic question: What was the aim of perestroika?

> The continual use of the army for unconstitutional ends raises a serious question. Whose side will the army take in the event of a civil confrontation? What's to become of the generals, who are jealous of their privileges and absolute power?

These words are from an open letter published in the newspaper *Komsomolskaya pravda* (Komsomol Truth) and signed by Volodya and other deputies and army officers in July 1990.

Until recently, Zolotukhin had been worried about the likelihood of a military coup. Now he thought the two hundred thousand homeless officers represented a greater threat. Ironically, an old disposition allowing generals to build themselves luxurious dachas at the state's expense was still in force.

When Volodya stepped forward for the parliamentary elections in 1989, Petya never thought his son would be elected deputy without either the blessing of the local Communist party leadership or the mandate of the military district of Turkestan. But Petya and the rival candidates had all underestimated the young man with the arrogant mustache who had no backers. Volodya had used a clever tactic. Speaking Russian to Russians and Uzbek to Uzbeks and using democratization as a unifying plank, he had been able to build bridges between the two communities.

Zolotukhin was elected deputy by those who wanted social change. He had enraged the Uzbek leadership, because political life in Tashkent still functioned according to the old authoritarian rules. Party heads, themselves tribal chiefs, laid down the norms of behavior, censored reformist publications from other republics, appointed directors of the media, and banned public demonstrations.

The Uzbek leadership had embraced nationalism. They asserted their independence vis-à-vis Moscow and were more disposed to grant concessions to Islam than to democracy. They tried to ignore Zolotukhin, boycotting him whenever they could. One day, the major found himself locked out of the office where he normally received his constituents; the next day, the theater where he had arranged to meet them instead was closed.

"Does this mean they're going to throw us out?" asked old Petya, realizing that—when it was a matter of his son's congressional seat—Volodya was obeying neither the Uzbek Communist Party leadership nor the army's Political Section. Through the latter, Volodya realized, the Soviet Communist Party controlled the officers' minds and monitored their ideological soundness. Zolotukhin backed military reform that would separate the

Communist party from the army. But until such reforms took place, his pragmatism told him that he must remain a Communist, which was why he continued working from within the party.

In Zolotukhin's view, soldiers should not sit in Parliament. He perceived his twin identity as an army officer and member of Congress as the product of a cross between a "Parliament made up of members from all walks of life, token milkmaids included," and a "Parliament of professional politicians." He knew he would have to make a choice between careers at any moment now, but for the time being he wanted to fight for a legal framework that would reestablish the harmony between the army and society. Military regulations that enslaved officers and deprived them of voluntary release or that exposed troops to the tyranny of their superiors had to be abolished.

In the Ministry of Defense, as in other Soviet institutions, a caste of officials had grown up who resisted change and defended their positions as dispensers of sinecures. Zolotukhin was tired of a patronage system that rewarded the "good" and punished the "wayward." He had been four years on the Army Political Section's list for a car. When his turn came, the car went to a captain. A car would have proved very handy in Moscow, but Volodya made no attempt to protest. He would buy himself one with his own money the day his salary reflected his job. At present, even by a generous estimate, his pay comes to about twenty-five dollars a month. Carless, he was deprived of the chance to earn extra money the way his friend Lieutenant Colonel Popov does, moonlighting as a pirate taxi driver.

The arbitrary decision about the car came as no surprise, for all of Tashkent's voices of dissent clustered around Major Zolotukhin. Mamura Khusanovna, his assistant, was the person who most irritated Uzbek Communist leaders, and they never lost a chance to ask Zolotukhin to fire her. She was his link with Birlik (Unity), the Uzbek nationalist movement, the first serious democratic opposition group to emerge in the republic. Compared with the nationalist movements of the Baltic or the Caucasus, Birlik took a middle-of-the-road line, but the Communists regarded it as one step away from heresy. Zolotukhin had very good relations with Birlik.

Khusanovna was head of Tumariz, the mothers' movement to protect young Uzbek army recruits. Over tea with the high command, these women were trying to bring about reforms in military service and the treatment of deserters. For one, the mothers did not want conscripts sent outside the republic and especially not into war zones. The group also wanted independent forensic reports on any Uzbek soldier who died outside the republic. The mothers asked that soldiers' coffins be opened and the identity of the corpses verified. Tashkent was only too familiar with these funereal consignments. The administration of the Afghan war had been centered in Tashkent: out of this city went food, medical supplies, soldiers, and newspapers; back to it came the bodies. For nearly a decade the corpses of Soviet soldiers killed in Afghanistan had been sent home in zinc coffins aboard a plane known in army slang as "The Black Tulip."

Afghanistan had been Zolotukhin's first assignment. After graduating from the military academy, in 1980, he spent six months covering the war as an army journalist for one of the many Soviet military newspapers and magazines. The Afghan war had begun in 1979, but Major Zolotukhin claims the worst years—those which saw the most casualties—were 1985 and 1986, when the Soviet regime stepped up the fighting, hoping for a decisive victory over the mujahedin. In Zolotukhin's view that decision, taken when Gorbachev was in power, "was senseless and cost many lives."

Afghanistan taught Volodya not to accept things blindly and sowed the seeds of doubt in his mind. If it had been a war of liberation, why were the casualty figures kept quiet, why were the Soviet sacrifices hidden? Out of what ambivalent shame had the room set aside for Afghanistan in the Tashkent Military Academy museum been kept secret?

Zolotukhin reminisced, "I had the illusion of taking part in a film that had nothing to do with me, of being in a dream or a hypnotic trance. I was numb. I took part in patrols and in mopping up operations. I scoured villages for guerrilla fighters and weapons. We did not understand that the men we came across were neither bandits nor extremists but people defending their families."

Years later, Zolotukhin felt indignation when Andrei Sakharov was booed in the Soviet Congress of Deputies. The academician had accused the military command of firing on Soviet soldiers in Afghanistan. Volodya refused to believe that any officer in his right mind would have given such an order, but neither could he accept it that deputies should react so crudely and with such a narrow sense of patriotism. After all, bungling was part and parcel of army life, and Zolotukhin himself had more than once come close to being the victim of a mistake.

Like many other young men, Zolotukhin hid from his parents the fact that he was in Afghanistan. He told them he was stationed at a frontier post where he could not be reached by telephone. Volodya regards his mother, who died of a heart attack a week after his return upon learning the truth, as one more victim of the war.

Before the USSR Supreme Soviet, Zolotukhin begged amnesty for soldiers who had committed crimes in Afghanistan. The courts had no right to judge criminal acts perpetrated in a war which itself was a criminal act. Without publicity and with the greatest discretion, Volodya devoted himself to the arduous task of tracking down the remaining Soviet prisoners of war, some dozens of men marooned in Afghanistan.

Until recently, Volodya had no concept of how vast the world was. It had broadened out before him in ever widening circles, which had reduced the family plot in Tashkent to a tiny speck. After Afghanistan he went to Moscow; then, in February 1990, he traveled to the West for the first time, where he was part of a parliamentary commission that visited NATO headquarters in Brussels. In his hotel room, remembering old Petya, Zolotukhin collected up all the miniature bottles from the small bar and took them home to his father. Petya was delighted with the tiny, different-colored bottles, and the contents of each tasted unlike anything he had ever drunk before.

With a much greater sense of diplomacy than his father or Aunt Valentina gave him credit for, Major Zolotukhin had used a recent trip to West Germany for a cause of his own. He wanted the Germans to build homes in Uzbekistan for Soviet soldiers in compensation for their withdrawal from East Germany. No one had sent Zolotukhin to West Germany, nor had anyone asked him to plead for anything. He had simply discovered for himself the art of lobbying and put it into practice of his own accord.

In the West, Zolotukhin became convinced that wealth is the fruit of work, and he discovered a talent for business. Now he wondered if this was compatible with his military uniform and his status as a deputy. Among several cherished projects was one to set up an independent news service for the whole of Central Asia.

Volodya had so enjoyed the West that he wanted to take his elder daughter Olya to Germany so that she, too, at the age of nine, would see that the world did not end at Tashkent or even at Moscow.

Zolotukhin wanted to broaden his horizons, to explore new countries and get to know new people. Wherever he was, however, an umbilical cord tied him to the family plot in Tashkent. "My homeland," he said, "is my house, my father, my wife, and my children." Volodya's homeland was, most of all, that leafy Tashkent garden that kept his childhood world alive in the eye of the hurricane.

Tashkent, 20 August 1990

3

■

Wallpaper

The tiny republic of Armenia, consisting of under twelve thousand square miles, is spiritual heir to one of the most ancient civilizations on earth. Surrounded by Muslim neighbors, Armenia is proud of its Christian tradition. The country has over three million people, 94 percent of them of Armenian origin. Coveted by Iran and Turkey, Armenia was conquered by the Red Army in 1920 and, together with Georgia and Azerbaijan, initially formed part of the Transcaucasian Federation, which was integrated into the Soviet Union in 1922. The current conflict between Armenia and Azerbaijan over Nagorno-Karabakh is the latest chapter in an old rivalry whose seeds were planted in 1919 and 1920, during another war for conquest of this territory. Yerevan, the Armenian capital, has over 1,215,000 inhabitants. Spitak, sixty miles to the north, was all but destroyed in the December 1988 earthquake. In 1990, 24,000 people were living there, several thousand of them Armenian refugees from Azerbaijan.

IT is two o'clock in the afternoon by the time our car sets out from Yerevan to Spitak, the Armenian town that was almost wiped off the map by an earthquake in December 1988. Now, in August, at this time of day, the heat is suffocating, and the landscape on either side of the road looks parched, scorched.

It was quite a struggle getting out of Yerevan. We were short of gasoline, to say nothing of a sense of organization. Besides, I was reluctant to return to Spitak, a place that held grim memories. I would rather have gone to the border of neighboring

Azerbaijan, where Armenian nationalist forces are guarding the frontier.

I blame myself for having succumbed to pressure from my companions instead of visiting border posts or making the rounds of the headquarters of the various armed bands presently swarming around Yerevan. My companions, Armenian patriots all, think that what a foreigner should see are the places destroyed by the earthquake. Their arguments are part religious, part blackmail. It is as if they were telling me that to refuse to visit Spitak would be showing disrespect for Armenia.

As our Zhiguli, a Soviet-built Fiat, races past trucks loaded with plywood panels and joists, I think about the sleepless Yerevan nights, so hot, so heavy with tensions, when a bullet fired from a checkpoint by a jittery gunman could end your life.

As darkness falls, my Armenian friends undergo a strange metamorphosis. By day they hold normal jobs as deputies to the Armenian Parliament, police chiefs, journalists, editors of Marxist publications, and Aeroflot pilots. By night, as if taking off masks, they shed their normal roles, and out come old family ties and intrigues, remnants of a tribal society that brings policemen, nationalist irregulars, and bandits together at a fraternal table under a grape arbor.

Instead of setting off for Spitak aboard our humble Zhiguli, I might have seen the command post of the ten members of the Armenian National Army (ANA) who last night made their way to the border in a stolen car. The ANA is yet another of the numerous armed groups that have sprung up since Armenia and Azerbaijan began clashing over the Nagorno-Karabakh region ("Artzakh," as the Armenians call it).

Soviet president Mikhail Gorbachev has not been able to disarm these irregular troops, but Levon Ter-Petrosian, the newly elected Armenian president, has told them to choose either to legitimize their status by becoming regulars or to remain beyond the pale and be declared outlaws. These are days of decision for the gunmen, and some of them are loathe to give up so quickly the niche they have carved out for themselves at gunpoint. To some extent, they look for conflict, sparking it off wherever they can, as if to justify their own lawless existence.

Razmik Vasilian, leader of the ANA, had promised to take me to the frontier, but then he got cold feet and withdrew the offer. Last night, in his headquarters, the atmosphere was feverish. Razmik's lieutenant, Hamlet, and the men were idly watching television in a room full of Kalashnikov rifles, automobile license plates, and Rambo posters. All at once, Razmik and his men began to stir, shouldered their guns, and, armed to the teeth, rushed out.

Owing to a cataract in one eye, Razmik has never done military service. He kisses his three-year-old son good-bye with a gun at his belt and a knife in his boot. Razmik is proudly awaiting the day when, on one of the rare occasions that he is at home, the boy will say, "Take me with you, Daddy."

As our car rounds the bends at full speed, I think about the militarization that has come to Armenia on the tail of its earthquake and economic crisis. I first visited Spitak in December 1988, immediately after the disaster. It was night, it was snowing, and Soviet armored troop carriers stood on the edge of Yerevan. I traveled in a battered truck, the last to dare make the trip from Zvardnotz airport to Spitak that day.

At the time, the headlights of oncoming cars lit up the faces of our driver and codriver, brothers-in-law who in their despair had several times made the awful journey there and back in the course of a day. The driver kept nodding off at the wheel, and his companion—despite not having slept for days—was still brazen enough to make a pass at me, no doubt in search of human warmth. I did not find it easy to ask him to keep his hands to himself. The earthquake had hurled him to the ground from four stories up and buried his whole family in the rubble. Now, under this blazing sun, I associate the memory of his eager, groping hands with the hands that fondle guns in Yerevan today.

On that night in December 1988, deep fissures split the earth on the outskirts of Spitak. The rough wooden coffins, scattered all about, were like a fleet of barges cast adrift. Bodies still lay beneath the rubble. Some of the survivors were eating canned sardines alongside bonfires, while others peered under the coffin lids in search of crushed and frozen relatives.

Today I ride in the backseat with Vazghen beside me. In front sit Klara and Suren, the driver. Vazghen has pledged his life to Armenia, vowing to return Nagorno-Karabakh to his country. At the foot of his bed in his modest house in Yerevan he has a map of Artzakh and a photo of Andrei Sakharov. Vazghen has about him the look of a monk. Dressed in black, he knows innumerable verses of Russian poetry by heart and recites them in a melancholy voice.

I like Vazghen, for he manages to avoid the response I most dread whenever I talk to a committed nationalist—the point when, lowering his voice, he asserts that his people are superior to anyone else and asks me whether I agree. Vazghen does not do this. He only asks me to play Armenian choral music when I sit down to write these lines and never to forget the trip we made one glorious evening to the famous Ghegard monastery dug out of the living rock by Armenians in the twelfth and thirteenth centuries.

Klara is an energetic, plumpish woman. Her hair is bleached, and she has long, varnished fingernails. The air blowing in through a side window balloons out the front of her low-necked dress, adding inches to her already large bust. It was she who had been most insistent on going to Spitak. Her brother is a leading figure in the Karabakh Committee, the militant nationalist group that was imprisoned immediately after the earthquake, when Moscow tried to prevent a rival government from being set up in Armenia. At the time, Klara acted bravely. She wrote letters to Gorbachev and went to Moscow to beg for her brother's freedom. As a result of this experience and of elections that gave power to the nationalists, Klara's family has become part of the new elite.

Portraits of Armenian military heroes, unearthed from the annals of history, line the highway. We pass cars with no license plates. They are stolen, mostly official, vehicles, "appropriated" for the Armenian cause.

My companions have little sense of time. We spent all morning hanging around, but are now speeding down the highway. Suren is ill, and just as we were about to leave for Spitak he insisted on stopping by the hospital. He wanted to give a bottle of brandy to the doctor who treated him when he began to lose the feeling in his lower extremities. Suren walks with a limp, and any hope of a cure lies beyond the borders of Armenia. Despite his leg pains, he drives at great speed and does not complain.

Suren and the others had prevailed upon Raphael, the police chief of a large Yerevan precinct, to help provide gasoline, which is scarce here. Raphael is a thick-set man with a hook nose and bushy eyebrows. His huge office has a table whose surface is completely bare. A smaller side table sports a battery of telephones, a microphone, an intercom, and a fax machine.

Despite the dozen or so devices at his disposal, Raphael is unable to communicate with anyone outside. He sweats, he shouts, and I imagine he is swearing in Armenian. Out of one of the many phones drifts a gloomy conversation between two women clinging to receivers somewhere in the city. The voices, courtesy of one of the chief's phones, take over the office, a comfortless place with a door that opens unexpectedly onto a refrigerator, a dining room, and a bed disguised as a bookcase.

Last night, as Raphael enjoyed a sumptuous meal under a leafy arbor, a policeman was shot dead by accident at a checkpoint. Raphael heard the news while we were in his office, and he thumped his fist on the table in outrage. Later, he jumped for joy at the news that two members of an armed gang that he regarded as enemies had been killed in a shoot-out not far from Yerevan. He is an emotional man and, according to what I have been told in confidence, extremely rich.

Some of Raphael's friends are at the Azerbaijan frontier, others patrol the hot streets of Yerevan by night with stolen weapons. Some people view Raphael as a patriot, others, as proof that a mafialike connection exists between a corrupt police force inherited from the past and armed freebooters, who loot and plunder behind a mask of patriotism.

Its tank full, thanks to Raphael, the Zhiguli tears along the highway playing a cassette of love songs by Vagram Tatukian. We had visited the folksinger, a friend of my traveling companions, in his home the night before. Vagram had been depressed after his foiled attempt to reach Ghetachen, an enclave of four thousand Armenians in Azerbaijan almost completely cut off by armed Azeris. The local military command would not allow Tatukian's helicopter to land.

Tatukian reserves his more tender lyrics to sing to his friends in his own living room. Here, surrounded by beautiful carpets, books on art and history, tapes of folk music, and songs by Charles Aznavour, Tatukian talks about his wife, who has emigrated to the United States. He still misses her very much. Reminders of her are everywhere: a wristwatch, her photograph, and, spread across a chair, a woman's blouse, which clearly was not worth taking all the way to America. Tatukian did not want to go, and he hopes she will come back. I am struck by the thought of this sensitive man one day singing his gentle songs and the next rushing off to the front to fight for a piece of land. In Ghetachen he boosts his fellow Armenians' morale with stirring songs of protest and resistance.

On the edge of Spitak is a hill topped by a church that looks as if it is made of aluminum. A vast cemetery, the graves of the earthquake victims, covers the hillside. Then come the homes of the survivors, a few of whom live in prefabricated houses erected by Italian and German relief teams. Most residents, however, occupy old railroad coaches, makeshift huts, and gasoline tank trailers, or else have settled back as best they can in the ruins.

Amid the devastation, Spitak's very ground still seems to tremble. A functioning refrigerator stands ringed by neat piles of rubble, as if the building that collapsed around it had risen out of the destruction, phoenixlike, in the form of this domestic appliance. Although deep in the aftermath of a disaster, people here are no worse off in their material lives than fellow Soviet citizens elsewhere.

Norik Muradian, First Secretary of the Communist Party of Spitak, is no stranger to the feeling of impotence. If life does not improve before the year is out, he will resign from the Soviet Congress and from his position as local party chief. Having worked in industry for more than thirty years, Norik does not want struggles against impossible odds to jeopardize his prestige as an effective administrator. He insists that he has seen little more than a fraction of the aid money that poured into Armenia from all over the world. Had he seen more, Norik would have started a poultry farm and a cement factory.

Even the ruins have fallen victim to implacable Soviet red tape. Cement deliveries to Spitak, still made on a quarterly basis, have been insufficient to rebuild the town. The precious commodity does not arrive, because trains into Armenia must first cross Azerbaijan, where they are stopped and looted. The Moscow government refuses to use force against the looters to ensure the convoys free passage. By holding back, the government is behaving like an imperial power on the brink of shedding a colony.

At first, it seemed as if the Soviet system had gone to extremes to help the earthquake victims. President Gorbachev had cut short a trip to the United States, and ministers in Moscow and authorities in the republics pledged their assistance. Yet none kept their word. The general upheaval in the USSR, coupled with growing mistrust among the republics, had squelched any enthusiasm for joining with Armenia in a common cause in the name of the old myth of friendship among the Soviet peoples.

"We're sorry, but our own republic's in so much trouble that we have to pull out," the Uzbek bricklayers told the Spitak party chief one day. According to Norik, Uzbeks could not be counted on. He remembered with some bitterness how Armenia had helped Uzbekistan when Tashkent was hit by an earthquake. That, however, had been years ago, when Armenians and Uzbeks were still members of one big family.

As if the earthquake were not enough, Norik has had to find housing for seven thousand Armenian refugees who fled to Spitak from Azerbaijan. The tremors struck at the height of this exodus. Five thousand people had escaped the threat of a pogrom only to die in a cataclysm here across the border.

Sometimes, says Norik, armed groups have turned up asking for contributions to the Armenian cause. "Get out of here; we've more than enough to cope with," he had to tell them. The men left without a fuss.

The moment we reach Spitak, Klara vanishes. After badgering everyone to come here, she does not go with us to the makeshift huts or the ruins. I am told she is at the lumberyard "drawing up a list." I assume she is making notes on which consumer items are in short supply, and I ask what is most urgently needed.

"That's not it," Suren says. "Klara's building herself a little place in the country, and she's gone to choose some wallpaper."

"Wallpaper?"

"You can't get wallpaper in Yerevan. But you can in Spitak," says Suren matter-of-factly.

Indignation rages in me like a storm. Buying up wallpaper from people who have nothing! Taking advantage of international solidarity just to decorate a vacation home!

Suren does not bat an eye. "What walls are they going to stick paper on around here?" he asks with cold logic.

I am nonplussed and do not know what to answer.

"Klara's new house is almost finished," he continues. "Isn't it better that she make the best of this opportunity?"

I fall silent. We leave town passing deeply fissured walls and clothes hanging out to dry in the sun. Taking no notice of their surroundings, men and women go about their daily tasks as they would in any other city in the world.

Klara does not return with us. I picture her studying different wallpaper samples, trying to imagine how they might look in her country cottage. Thanks to the earthquake, Klara is able to turn a small corner of her beloved Armenia into a cozy living room. Her Spitak wallpaper affirms her indomitable will, even if what stands between her and desolation is nothing more than a bit of floral print.

Yerevan, 17 August 1990

4

---∎---

A Provincial Newspaperwoman

The industrial city of Rezh, in the province of Sverdlovsk, was founded under Catherine the Great in the latter half of the eighteenth century. Rezh grew out of one of the many industrial villages that sprang up close to the iron and coal deposits discovered in the Ural region during the sixteenth century. A large part of Rezh's present population of fifty-one thousand works in the defense industry, which kept the town closed to foreigners until 1991. Today, the economic crisis and environmental pollution are two of the serious problems that face the city. Rezh is located fifty miles from Ekaterinburg—the old name of the city of Sverdlovsk, restored after the failed coup of August 1991—the provincial capital.

TATYANA Merzlyakova ran *Kommunisticheskaya pravda* (The Communist Truth), a newspaper that appeared three or four times a week in Rezh, a small city in the Urals. She had not been doing badly. Since her appointment as editor in January 1989 she had managed to boost the paper's circulation to fifteen thousand, no mean figure in a place with a population of barely over fifty thousand. Even so, Tatyana was not satisfied. The paper's title barred it from real commercial success.

Tatyana tried to convince local party officials that Communist truth was hardly enhanced by the fact that under this banner they were publishing photos of down-at-heel tramps who lived off what they scavenged from rubbish dumps. Her arguments were of no avail. Not for a minute were the party bigwigs willing to consider changing the paper's name. Especially not to some-

thing like the proposed *The Four Winds,* which smacked of a
whole raft of heretical ideologies, not to mention crypto-plural-
ism and editorial caprice. But Tatyana refused to give up.

It was July 1990, and Tatyana was in Moscow. She had been
elected delegate to the Soviet Communist Party's Twenty-eighth
Congress, one of the high points in her life. At the congress she
was appointed secretary to the editorial staff of *Microphone
Number 13,* a magazine compiled by a group of delegates, journalists, and other enthusiasts. *Microphone Number 13* was very
important to Tatyana, since it enabled her for the first time to
test her strength against the cream of the Soviet newspaper and
magazine world: men like Yegor Yakovlev, editor of the weekly
Moscow News, Otto Latsis, assistant editor of *Komunist,* the
Marxist-Leninist review, and Yury Chernichenko, the agricultural columnist, who pitted his considerable erudition against
the system of sovkhozy and kolkhozy. Agriculture was Tatyana's
soft spot.

She had insisted on paying her Communist party dues to the
cell of a sovkhoz, stating openly that had there been viable al-
ternatives to the Communist party she would have joined a peasant party. She emphasized that she meant a party of ordinary
peasants, not of presidents of kolkhozy or sovkhozy—such as
Vasily Starodubtsev, who was still committed to building communism in rural areas—or of those who wanted to redistribute
the land in tracts to be cultivated by tenants or run as private
farms.

Tatyana claimed repeatedly that she was a "provincial." She
stated this to explain away her loud outfits, floral prints so unlike
the casual dress of her colleagues on the *Moscow News.* She also
said it to defuse any possible criticism and, moreover, to accen-
tuate her good points. Out of her mouth the word sounded a
lively, promising note from the very heart of Russia.

Tatyana belongs to that army of journalists fighting to bring
glasnost to the provinces. The scope of her freedom has been
more restricted than that of her Moscow counterparts. Stuck in
a more conservative and primitive society, she has had to con-

front certain local party chiefs who are used to blind obedience from their underlings. After editing four issues of *Microphone Number 13* and working for two weeks alongside some of the party's best journalists, she found it difficult to return to the petty routine and wrangling of Rezh. The Twenty-eighth Congress was the most important event in Tatyana's life.

As far as getting ahead was concerned, Tatyana saw herself at the age of thirty-three as a perfect fulfillment of the tenets of communism. She had been born in the middle of Asia, in a small village in the Altay region, where her mother was a nurse and her father a truck driver. From an early age she had excelled at writing. She had fine teachers, for although she attended a small village school, some of its staff were intellectuals who had been evacuated from Leningrad during the war. They had stayed on, to be joined by others wanting to start a new life in a place that was looking for settlers.

In her last year of high school, Tatyana was editor of the student paper. Her teacher wanted her to become a journalist, but the nearest school of journalism was in the city of Sverdlovsk. Considered one of the three best in the Soviet Union at the time, it accepted only a limited number of students.

Tatyana would have enrolled in a teacher training college near her home had it not been for her first boyfriend, whom she still refers to as "my first love." He had been opposed to her choosing the easier path. "To this day I'm grateful to my first love for what he did," Tatyana said from the armchair in her hotel room, where she sat sipping tea.

Tatyana studied in Sverdlovsk and graduated with distinction during the period when Boris Yeltsin was first secretary of the local party. The label she put on those years—"the period of growing stagnation"—was a contradiction in terms. She learned Lenin by heart and never regretted it, since it was handy to be able to quote him whenever the need arose. Tatyana could rattle off Lenin's advice to the journalists of the Revolution as if she were in a Communist Youth camp or receiving a prize at high school graduation.

In Rezh, where she moved in 1978, Tatyana began work as a farming reporter. Her speciality was "places without a future." This was the name given to villages that were being deliberately starved of funds to make way for new artificial regional centers. To force the inhabitants out more quickly, the authorities were slowly cutting off the few available services.

Tatyana wrote articles calling for the reopening of a school, a clinic, or a bus stop. These were her little triumphs. Now with the new agrarian legislation, perhaps, if the idea of parceling out land among individual peasants caught on, these badly treated villages—which had never recovered from collectivization or the war—might at last have a future. One of the first things that Tatyana wanted to do, if allowed, was to install telephones everywhere.

By 1989 Tatyana knew most people around Rezh down to the last dairymaid, and just when she was getting bored she was offered the job of editing *The Communist Truth*, the official organ of the Rezh Communist Party and soviet. It was a four-page tabloid, first published in 1930, whose motto was "Workers of the world, unite!"

Choosing a woman to run *The Communist Truth* had been the brainchild of the secretary of the local party committee, or *gorkom*. Tatyana was astonished, not only because in the Soviet Union it was unusual for a woman to become editor of a newspaper but also because there had been two men higher up the ladder than she, in both seniority and experience.

Tatyana told the committee secretary she would think it over. She was someone who spoke her mind, and she was not going to let that be changed. This pronouncement was exactly what the new secretary wanted to hear. The editorial board put Tatyana to the test. Three weeks after she was appointed, they handed her an article that fiercely criticized the president of the municipal executive committee, or *gorispolkom*. At first, thinking her fellow editors were trying to trick her, she did not dare publish it. Then she reconsidered. The article, after all, only told the truth. When she published it, there was no adverse reaction. So Tatyana began to publish more news and less ideology.

Phone calls started pouring in from the party committee members. "What's going on, Tatyana Georgievna? Why aren't we getting any more of our usual editorials?" They were referring to the customary heavy-handed ideological slant.

"People need news, and ideology can be presented through the news," replied Tatyana. The problem was that the Rezh party committee included an ideological section, which somehow or other had to justify its existence.

In the Soviet parliamentary elections of March 1989 Tatyana got a chance to clinch her editorship of *The Communist Truth*. She did not support the official candidate, whose excessive campaign featured a group of folk dancers and a theater company. Instead, she did her utmost to back his opponent, an engineer who was an unknown quantity. The official candidate lost, and Tatyana found herself having to confront the full Rezh committee of the Soviet Communist Party, who had the right to fire her.

"I didn't give in. I didn't grovel. I told them if they didn't like the paper they could find another editor," Tatyana explained.

The committee did not fire her, and a few months later, when figures showed that *The Communist Truth*'s circulation had grown from thirteen thousand to fifteen thousand, they stopped bothering her. But the nagging problem of the paper's name would not go away, so Tatyana asked its readership to vote on the matter. After all, there was a precedent. Until 1953 the paper had been called *The Bolshevik*. Now, however, a lack of unanimity among Tatyana's readers allowed the *gorkom* to drag its feet. The only concession Tatyana managed to win from them was to replace the logo "Workers of the world, unite!" with "Democracy for Russia." This, at least, was something.

Tatyana joined the party in December 1985, a move she had not been particularly eager to make prior to Gorbachev's ascent to power. Under Gorbachev, she thought, the party might become more than just a springboard to a career.

"There was a new spirit of freedom in the party, that's why I joined. Sometimes now I'd like to get out, but I hate to turn my back on Gorbachev's party."

The idea of leaving the party occurred to Tatyana when she found the secretaries of the Communist party regional committees, the *obkomi,* criticizing reformers like the veteran Aleksandr Yakovlev or the leaders of the Democratic Platform movement. "Being in the same party as the *obkomi* people bothers me," she said. "But if I leave who'll take them on?"

The Communist Truth could hardly avoid dealing with the subject of privilege. In a society beset by hunger and poverty, a privilege might amount to no more than the gift of a piece of meat. On the eve of May Day, a reader—described by Tatyana as "well-meaning"—telephoned to blow the whistle on members of the *gorispolkom,* who were receiving hampers of champagne, caviar, fish, candy, and meat. Letters about the iniquity were published in *The Communist Truth,* and readers greeted the news with indignation. Thereafter the hampers ceased. Thanks to the paper, Rezh's party leaders have had to suffer the same deprivations as their fellow citizens, not that this gave the latter much comfort.

It was hot in Moscow, and Tatyana had changed her outfit with the floral jacket for slippers and a housecoat. She was feeling homesick. Her nine-year-old daughter and her husband, the head of the Rezh judiciary, were waiting for her at home. Tatyana had married during her fifth year at university. "I wouldn't say he was the love of my life, but he was so devoted to me that when he got sent to Rezh I couldn't break off with him. He'd never have found a wife in Rezh, so I went with him." There had been only one love in her life, Tatyana reminded me—the first. "Such a pure, platonic, romantic love. We kissed on the cheek, and that was all."

Where Tatyana had been brought up, modesty and respectability had been all-important womanly virtues. She cited the example of her grandmother, who saw her husband off to the front in 1941. In 1945, a few months after he returned seriously wounded, she watched him die. "At thirty-one," the grand-mother had said, "I was left on my own, and after that I never once opened the door to a strange man—and all men were strange."

The subjects of sex and morality were very much on Tatyana's mind and kept coming up in our conversation. In the hot Moscow night air, she talked about provincial taboos.

"I don't consider it normal," Tatyana said, declaring her position, "but among us it's unusual for a woman to go with a man before marriage." For her, to have "gone" with someone before her wedding would have been nothing short of a "tragedy." Her husband had confessed that before they were married he had entertained "certain ideas" but had been careful not to put them into practice, fearing that Tatyana "might kill herself." Tatyana, he thought, was like her grandmother.

"If my daughter sleeps with someone before she's married, it won't be a tragedy for me, even though I'd rather she didn't," Tatyana explained. "But it would be for my husband. He'd throw us both out of the house. In that sense, he's old-fashioned."

Although committed to glasnost, Tatyana has her limitations. She allows trainee reporters to write about anything "except erotic subjects." Even though the atmosphere is more open now, she informs them, she is still quite conventional.

"I let them publish anything, even interviews with Democratic Union extremists, if that's what they feel like doing. Anything but eroticism. But what they want is a bare bosom in every issue." The Democratic Union she refers to is a vehemently anti-Communist opposition group.

Tatyana's limitations became evident in April 1990, when she had occasion to interview Raisa Maximovna Gorbacheva during the first lady's visit to the province of Sverdlovsk. The interview, entitled "An Informal Meeting," appeared on 1 May. Rezh, with its industrially polluted air, was not on Raisa's itinerary, but she insisted on stopping there. As a girl during the war, she had lived in Alapayevsk, a nearby city, where her father worked on the

railroad. This was one time when Tatyana Merzlyakova prac-
ticed self-censorship. Knowing it would displease the paper's
readers, she did not dare appear overly cordial to Raisa Maximovna. "We aren't used to reporting on the first lady and her
travels around the country. I was afraid to write about some of
the subjects she mentioned, so I didn't say she'd asked for support for Mikhail Sergeivich, and I left out her remarks about the
difficulties perestroika was encountering."

Tatyana had tried to strike a compromise between her personal respect for Raisa and the paper's reputation, especially
since the interview was being published in the home territory of
Boris Yeltsin, the man who was nipping at the Soviet leader's
heels. Fawning over Gorbachev—or worse, over his wife, whose
frequent changes of costume irritated the Russians—was not in
the interests of *The Communist Truth*.

In September 1990, Tatyana was back in Moscow. She was
undecided whether to remain in the party. *The Communist Truth*
was now called *Rzhevskaya vest* (The Rezh News) and had been
registered in accordance with the new press laws that came into
force on 1 August, but this change did little to cheer up Tatyana.
Censorship had been abolished, but market forces were now a
cruel factor in the media world.

Tatyana had confronted another truth that was not that of
communism: newsprint, ink, and distribution costs had risen
drastically. She did all she could to contest the terms imposed by
the Ministry of Communications. In 1990 the ministry had
charged three thousand rubles to distribute the paper, but by the
next year it was asking for thirty-two thousand—even after, as
Tatyana said, she had got down on her knees and pleaded with
the local postmaster, a further humiliation, for he was only "a
former mailman."

Perhaps these price increases were a plot trumped up by
"forces" that wanted to put glasnost out of business. "Each copy
of the paper costs three kopecks, out of which the ministry keeps
two-thirds. We won't get subsidies anymore. They didn't amount

to much—fifteen thousand rubles a year—but that went some way. We carried out some renovations. We wanted to build an apartment for our photographer, but now we're going to take losses."

Tatyana's outlook had changed. If she wanted to be independent, she was going to have to raise capital for the paper. To her, a free-market economy seemed more to be feared than the party.

"The party's no bother to a tough journalist. The most its leaders can do is phone and give me their views. That's all. But now that I'm dependent on money, we'll see just how tough I am. When it comes to money, he who pays the piper calls the tune. I'm determined to raise it. I'm going to fight the Ministry of Communications tooth and nail to make it lower its charges, and we'll look for new sources of income."

Tatyana was reviewing the situation. She was prepared to publish anything from pages of household hints to volumes of poetry. Anything, that is, except sex.

Moscow, July–September 1990

5

Founders

The beautiful city of Yaroslavl is on the right bank of the Volga, about 160 miles northeast of Moscow. Capital of the province of the same name, Yaroslavl is an important river port and is also located on the rail line to Archangel. Yaroslavl was founded in the eleventh century and four hundred years later became part of the principality of Moscow. Today the Volga city has close to 750,000 inhabitants and is a center of the heavy machinery, chemical, and oil refining industries. Despite its many factories, Yaroslavl's character is still determined by the six-teenth- and seventeenth-century buildings that shape its distinctive sky-line. Conspicuous among these are the monastery of Spaso-Preobra-zhenski and the Ilia Prorok (Elijah the Prophet) church. The city's collection of frescoes and icons is one of the most outstanding in Russia. In the south of the province's fourteen thousand square miles are the old Russian cities of Rostov, Uglich, and Pereslavl-Zalesski, which are preserved as historic monuments.

ONE rainy Friday toward the end of August 1990, Georgy Fyodorovich took a small overnight bag, his toothbrush, and four bundles of freshly printed newspapers and went to Yaroslavl to found a branch of a new political party.

Georgy Fyodorovich Khatsenkov was vice-president of the Democratic Party of Russia (DPR), an organization more widely known as "Travkin's party," after Nikolai Travkin, the DPR's president and an outspoken worker, or "Kasparov's party," after the chess grand master Garri Kasparov, one of the party's prin-cipal backers.

Like Travkin and Kasparov, Georgy Fyodorovich also had left the Soviet Communist Party a short while before. But Georgy's was a special case. For the previous four years he had earned his living as a member of the apparat, or party bureaucracy, of the Central Committee, writing speeches and reports for its top leaders and forums. On occasion, Khatsenkov's sentences were lumped together with those of a dozen other colleagues, and the anonymous mishmash would appear in the press as a policy statement reflecting the latest political position.

Khatsenkov knew only too well how ruthless Communist scribes were with words they found suspect. Terms like "private property" or "market economy" or "democracy," or even "human face," were twisted, watered down, or simply banned. Fearing both the words and the ideas associated with them, the apparatchiks tinkered away at an offending expression until they had rendered it meaningless.

As controversy raged during preparations for the party's Twenty-eighth Congress, Khatsenkov took the daring step of trying to organize a discussion group in the party's inner sanctum at its Old Square headquarters, in Moscow. The idea bombed. Meanwhile, the rear guard—whose job it had been to eradicate heretical words from speeches—still hoped to carry out a purge and cleanse the party of deviationist elements. To this end, it decided to investigate Khatsenkov. During the questioning, no record of which was made, Georgy Fyodorovich asked his inquisitors why they did not open his skull to see whether his nerve endings went "left or right." The party was not capable of reforming itself, Georgy now saw, nor were its internal dissidents likely to achieve anything in the battles they hoped to wage at the Twenty-eighth Congress. Accordingly, in the spring of 1990 he resigned.

By March 1990 the Soviet Parliament had abolished Article Six of the Constitution, which gave the Communist party the leading role in government. Although this action removed the last formal obstacle to a multiparty system, months later it was still not possible to register groups that aspired to become political parties. This situation allowed them no chance to become known in the vast Soviet hinterland, let alone test their real strength in an electoral contest. Lacking the permanent infrastructure enjoyed by the Communists, these groups subsisted on the fringes and in the gaps left vacant by the party.

Despite legal restrictions, a number of these organizations— among them the Democratic Party of Russia—set out in the summer of 1990 to found branches in the provinces. Imbued with missionary zeal, their leaders embarked on exhausting reconnaissance tours, which brought them face to face with the reality of a brutalized provincial Russia.

Because he had a cold and did not feel up to coping with the muddy country roads, Georgy Fyodorovich had decided to take the train to Yaroslavl. Neither he nor Sasha, his burly bodyguard who was armed with a revolver, had ever been there before, although the beautiful city—the epitome of the soul of Russia— is less than two hundred miles from Moscow.

To Georgy Fyodorovich it must have seemed an age since the days when he traveled around Uzbekistan in the comfortable backseat of a black Chaika. In that not-really-so-distant past, Central Asia's Communist leaders had trembled at the arrival of this balding, bespectacled man whose mandate—on behalf of the Soviet Communist Party Central Committee—was to stick his nose into everything.

Communists in the provinces saw Georgy Fyodorovich as the "inspector" from Moscow, and Asiatic party leaders had their own standards of hospitality. They regaled him with sumptuous dinners; they invited him to their official residences, swimming pools, and gardens; they sent him masseurs; and, sometimes, they placed luxurious gifts in his room.

When this happened, Georgy Fyodorovich would react in line with Moscow's most recent political tack, news of which had not yet reached the provinces. Accordingly, if necessary, to dispel any notion that he might be open to bribery, the following day he would see to it that some provincial official's head rolled.

Georgy Fyodorovich was recounting all this as the train pulled into Yaroslavl, where Lev Rastegaev, president of the Yaroslavl Popular Front, stood waiting. This unusually phlegmatic character, who sported a thick beard, was a radio and television repairman. He had prepared the way for the Democrats to take over the Popular Front, a political group on its last legs.

The Yaroslavl Popular Front had been prestigious during the early years of perestroika, but the 1990 municipal elections had shown that in Russia such broad-based democratic organizations had nothing like the support they enjoyed in the Baltic republics. It was going to be hard to get an alternative political system off the ground in Yaroslavl.

From the vantage point of 1990, the 1987 Popular Front successes, which brought thousands out into the streets in protest against Communist party decisions and rejected its provincial leaders, seemed insignificant alongside the fact that the reins of power remained in Communist hands. Worse, the people of Yaroslavl in 1990 had sunk into apathy and were less keen to take part in demonstrations. They were disillusioned with "democrats" even before these had been given a chance to prove their worth.

Complaining that his head and nose were becoming more and more congested, Georgy Fyodorovich went on with his story about how an official black car would come to pick him up at the airport and take him straight to this or that party residence, where an invigorating hot dinner awaited him. With a twinkle in his eye, he told us how he particularly enjoyed working in Central Committee dachas on the outskirts of Moscow, where he was given comfortable rooms, treated to sauna baths and tennis games, and looked after by attentive waiters.

How are the mighty fallen, Comrade Khatsenkov!

It was cold and wet in Yaroslavl as the streetcar bore Georgy Fyodorovich and his companions through the dark streets to the main square. The vehicle, with its cargo of glum, ill-tempered people loaded down with bundles and smelling of sour cabbage, seemed to be carrying us backward in time through a landscape dotted with bell towers, onion-domed churches, crumbling walls,

and nineteenth-century merchants' mansions. Ahead, beyond or-
namental iron railings, the majestic Volga cast its enchantment
over the torpid city.

Georgy Fyodorovich was in a crabby mood, regretting that
he had not brought a warm jacket. The hotel could not find our
room reservations and did not want to accept our passports.
Georgy Fyodorovich's failed to list his new Moscow address,
where he had moved after leaving the luxury apartment he had
occupied as a member of the staff serving the Central Committee.
That apartment had been in a complex built of the best bricks
and materials the party could commandeer. The place had been
carefully finished, which distinguished it from the general run of
apartment blocks, with their crooked wall switches, their dingy
stairways, and their shabby elevators. In the elevators of the
Central Committee's buildings, children did not pee in the corridors and adults did not spit on the walls. Only a few days
before our trip, Georgy Fyodorovich had moved into a small,
dirty old place in the middle of the city. On returning from her
vacation, Georgy Fyodorovich's wife almost passed out when he
confronted her with the fait accompli.

"Sometimes we have to get nearer to the people, darling," he
reasoned, and in case this argument was not enough he gave her
a more compelling one. "The day the people go on the rampage
and begin helping themselves to the party's belongings, they're
sure to make a beeline for Novocheryomushkinskaya Street,
where they will take no pity on apparatchiks. So it's better to
get out now, darling."

Georgy Fyodorovich was generally a jovial man and, in view
of the times, had a surprising zest for life. It may have been part
of his nature; it may have been a hangover from the easy world
in which he had recently been wallowing. I thought the former
more likely, since he had not been an apparatchik for very long.
When he was elevated to the staff of the Central Committee in
1986, he was already "full of enthusiasm and hope that things
would change."

The Hotel Yaroslavl's restaurant had closed by the time

Georgy Fyodorovich finished registering. We had no choice but to make do with some sardine patties that, out of a cunning born of hunger, Sasha the bodyguard and I managed to purloin from the dining room out of the remains of a wedding feast. We already had a bottle of vodka and some pimientos in garlic that Sasha's thoughtful wife had provided.

We drank to the health of the party that was to be founded the next day. This reminded Georgy Fyodorovich of the days when on behalf of the Central Committee, with a stiff brandy or two at his elbow, he penned diatribes against drinking. His arguments delighted Yegor Ligachev, the Politburo's standard-bearer in its anti-alcohol campaign and its war on illicit stills. What would Ligachev be drinking now?

His hands greasy with sardine oil, Georgy Fyodorovich waxed nostalgic about the last trout he had dined on in Karlovy Vary, the deluxe Czech resort that was such a favorite with the Communist elite. He remembered how he had once bumped into Viktoria Brezhneva, the widow of the former Soviet premier, there in the lobby of the Hotel Bristol. What would become of those spas now, with all the rooms that used to be reserved for fellow Communist party officials? Another wave of nostalgia washed over Georgy Fyodorovich when he recalled the beer he had consumed in Karlovy Vary in the intervals between sipping its mineral waters.

Lev Rastegaev raised his glass to the success of the DPR's Constituent Assembly and quickly walked away down the dark street. He had things to do, maybe a family expecting him home, and party matters are not personal matters. He took with him three of the bundles of newspapers. The *Demokraticheskaya gazeta* was the party's chief means of support.

The organization that Georgy Fyodorovich had gone to Yaroslavl to found claimed to be the leading Russian party after the Communists. Half a million membership cards had been ordered, and by the autumn the new group hoped to have one million members. They looked on Boris Yeltsin, president of the

Supreme Soviet of the Russian Federation, as a member in secret, especially because Gennady Burbulis, Yeltsin's personal envoy, was one of the DPR's leaders. (Later that year, Burbulis left the DPR on the grounds that the post was incompatible with his job as Yeltsin's representative.)

As Georgy Fyodorovich saw it, the DPR was a liberal party short on slogans and rhetoric. It called on all democratic forces to unite in bringing about the "constitutional overthrow of the Soviet Communist Party apparat." The DPR deliberately shunned social-democratic concepts, even Swedish ones, in order to focus on the freedom of the individual, economic competition, and the free market. Georgy Fyodorovich looked forward to the day when it would be possible to set up a publishing consortium in Russia like the German firm of Springer, buy a period mansion in Yaroslavl, and open a branch of the DPR there. And that night, with these apostolic dreams, he fell asleep.

The next day, after a light breakfast, Georgy Fyodorovich, Sasha, and I got back on the streetcar. The DPR's Constituent Assembly was to hold its first meeting some distance from the center of the city in a suburban venue borrowed for the occasion. Two hundred people were in attendance, about a hundred of whom on that Saturday in August were to become the core of the party.

Georgy Fyodorovich made the opening speech in the pragmatic style that was his hallmark. "The state is falling apart," he said. "We must create a structure that will save us from the collective grave this regime is digging itself. We must fight to prevent the regional first secretaries of the Communist party from grabbing all the jobs. We must put an end to the Communist party's monopoly of power—not by copying their methods but by employing constitutional means."

The delegates showed more interest in Khatsenkov's Communist past than in the political message he was trying to convey, however, and they kept asking him questions about his activities as a member of the Central Committee apparat. Khatsenkov insisted that he had never been a dyed-in-the-wool apparatchik but rather a foreign body, a sort of virus, in the Central Committee's offices.

True to his vision of the future, Khatsenkov urged the DPR's faithful to buy a printing office or an old house. "Buy, buy! We'll back you up," he told the founders of the Yaroslavl DPR as they counted out their coins to pay for their lunches at a nearby canteen, whose humble menu featured vegetable soup, meat and potatoes, plus jam and tea at three rubles and seventy kopecks.

"The man's a chameleon. I don't trust him. If he was a devoted supporter of Marx and Lenin under the Communists, how do we know he's sincere now?" one delegate muttered between mouthfuls.

After lunch, the assembly went on to discuss one of the thorny issues of the day—house ownership. The first steps toward this eventuality had already been taken in Moscow, but actual privatization was not to start until the autumn of 1991.

"What about those of us who've been waiting for a house for the last fifteen years? Are we supposed to buy one now?" a delegate asked.

A crippled pensioner in a soaking wet beret, a dozen medals adorning his jacket, mounted the rostrum with the help of his cane. Describing himself as a man who had "seen it all except for the Revolution and the Civil War," the old veteran gave the delegates a piece of advice. "Our past excesses stem from the fact that communism is utopian and therefore dangerous for us and the rest of the world."

Earlier that summer, a scarcity of tobacco had brought the people of Yaroslavl into the streets in a way that no new political movement could have done. Overnight the city's smokers became the vanguard of social change. During a nationwide cigarette shortage, a number of workshops in the local car factory, which employed forty thousand workers, had called a two-day strike. Deprivation of a simple source of pleasure was all it had taken to make them form a strike committee, something their politically minded co-workers had been trying vainly to do for two years. The men had asked for a daily package of cigarettes, an end to paying party dues, and a program of transition to a market economy.

At our DPR meeting, speakers got up one after another, flitting from theme to theme, and the audience listened as closely to those who did not talk sense as to those who did.

"The rest of you may not know it," an elderly woman told the assembly, pointing at the man at the podium, "but the speaker's sick in the head."

"How could we have known?" another woman, several rows behind, called out. "Are we psychiatrists?"

Only when it was absolutely necessary did Georgy Fyodorovich break in to steer the discussion. "You are creating a structure," he reminded them. "And experience shows that it will grow—just as if you'd put yeast in it. You'll be astonished."

Evening came. A steering committee had still to be appointed and the first resolutions approved before we could return to Moscow. Candidates introduced themselves. They said little, barely giving more than their names, ages, and professions, plus one other crucial detail—their relationship with the Communist party. Some, who had never been members, said so loud and clear; others, seeing how it would count in their favor, said, "I never joined, even though I was asked to on a number of occasions."

Those who had been members made acts of contrition and explained when and why they had demeaned themselves. Each date of entry or exit from the party had a different standing in the new scale of moral values. To have left after the Twenty-eighth Congress that summer was worth less than to have done so earlier, when it took greater courage. The worst transgression was to have belonged to the opposition within the party itself, for such a stand suggested that the candidate in question had harbored the treacherous hope that the Communist organism could be brought back to life.

Once elected, the steering committee began to discuss the first proposals before the Yaroslavl DPR. These were a vote of censure for the way local authorities had organized the harvest and a statement of support for a member of a cooperative jailed for insulting a local police chief.

To whom should they address their complaints about agricultural policy in the area? The executive committee? The regional soviet? Those who had elected the regional soviet? Crops that year had been very good, so good that a state of emergency had been declared in order to mobilize people for the harvest. Ordinary citizens had participated halfheartedly, though, for the days were gone when people would pitch in and fight the "battle of the harvest" without being paid for their time. As in other years, the cabbages had been transported by bus and truck. Local deputy Adelaida Besheva, who was now taking part in the founding of the DPR, had also obeyed the call, for, when all was said and done, in the Soviet Union the word "harvest" was sacred. Adelaida Besheva and her political team worked a whole day in a cucumber patch. That night, muscles aching, she lay on her living room sofa, unable even to go and collect the carrots that were payment for all her hard work.

"Keep away from that," shouted Khatsenkov from the podium. "Let the Communists go out into the fields. We must give land to the farmers and stop these harvest battles. Our problems are more fundamental."

The case of the jailed cooperative member was more clear-cut. Here the new party could show its muscle. "We have a chance to make some political capital here," Georgy Fyodorovich said.

The party founders next looked into the planning of a municipal shadow government. Georgy Fyodorovich was of the view that the DPR was not yet strong enough for such a step and could easily make itself look ridiculous. It turned out, in any case, that a shadow cabinet was already in existence. Other opposition groups had set it up. All the DPR could do was to decide whether or not it wanted to be part of that body. Lev Rastegaev, in fact, had given it his approval.

Georgy Fyodorovich was skeptical. Let others get their fingers burned, he said. The bemedaled veteran agreed. To get mixed up in a power struggle now was "sticking our necks in the guillotine before we have to."

"We must do something concrete!" Georgy Fyodorovich exhorted. "Otherwise people will say that under previous governments they at least had bread."

The Yaroslavl branch of the Democratic Party of Russia had been duly constituted. Rastegaev, who had received the most votes, became its president. The founders clapped, congratulated themselves, and began to leave the hall. With that, the organizers of the event returned to its center-stage position the imitation marble bust of Lenin that had been discreetly carried into the wings before the assembly gathered.

For Georgy Fyodorovich it was time to return to Moscow. His cold had made great strides in Yaroslavl.

Yaroslavl, 24–25 August 1990

6

The Last Battle

Forests and oil are the chief natural wealth of the region of Tomsk, a territory in western Siberia with an area of over 115,000 square miles and a population of a little more than one million. The regional capital, Tomsk, Siberia's oldest city, was founded by Cossacks in 1604 as a fortress on the right bank of the river Tom, a tributary of the Ob. In the nineteenth century, Tomsk became a prosperous trading center as well as the seat of the first university to be founded in Asiatic Russia. Owing to its nuclear industries, which served the Soviet defense program, the city of Tomsk was out of bounds to foreign visitors until the end of 1990. The Kolomenskie Grivy sovkhoz, the region's largest, is located on the Ob, about 150 miles north of Tomsk. The village of Kolomenskie Grivy, with its thousand or so inhabitants, lies within the sovkhoz.

THE final strains of *The Internationale* were still echoing through the Kremlin's Palace of Congresses, but many of the party delegates—trying to avoid the long lines outside the cloakrooms—had begun to walk out before the anthem finished. A drizzle was falling on Moscow, and the coatracks bulged with raincoats. Some of the delegates hoped to catch planes that night for distant points in the depths of Russia.

Like everyone else, Rembert Paloson wanted to return home. He lived in the Siberian province of Tomsk, almost two thousand miles from Moscow, in an idyllic spot among birches and firs on the banks of the river Ob. But it never occurred to Paloson to leave the congress before the end. Trained to remain until the last notes of *The Internationale* died away, he stayed on now to listen to Mikhail Gorbachev, Secretary General of the Soviet Communist Party, even though Paloson believed that—like the anthem—Gorbachev had lost the power to hold an audience. It was 6 September 1990, the day that concluded the second stage of the Russian Communist Party's Constituent Assembly.

Paloson is a conservative, one of those representatives of Soviet socialism whom reformist politicians rail against. Advocates of a new agrarian policy aimed at bringing a market economy and private property into rural areas of the Soviet Union find in him the embodiment of all they most hate. Paloson is head of a sovkhoz, the state farm which, together with the kolkhoz, or collective farm, has formed the basis of Soviet agriculture since the days of Stalinist collectivization. Worse still, he is in charge of the biggest and richest sovkhoz in Tomsk, Kolomenskie Grivy, and this endows him with the objective basis and "moral right" from which to argue in favor of this kind of farming.

Paloson is a man who believes in the socialist system, in its capacity to perfect itself and make justice prevail over any form of arbitrariness. He has never lost this faith and looks on his own life as proof that the system is ultimately fair. He counts himself a longtime close friend of Yegor Ligachev, the Communist boss who until the summer of 1990 was the implacable scourge of the reformists. The two men's friendship dates from the period when Ligachev was First Secretary of the Tomsk Communist Party, a post he held from 1965 to 1983. At that time, Leonid Brezhnev was at the country's helm. In Tomsk, a province half the size of Texas and a long way from Moscow, Ligachev was "building socialism" by sheer energy and willpower. Paloson was among his faithful allies.

Paloson and Ligachev like and respect each other. In Ligachev's eyes, Paloson is living confirmation that "Soviet man" is possible. For many Muscovite liberals, Ligachev is a bogeyman, a holdover from authoritarian, bureaucratic socialism. Even so, Paloson regards Ligachev as an honest man, someone endowed with an enormous capacity for work, a comrade, and a friend. The two men are perhaps better defined in terms of age than of ideology. They are hale and hearty old-timers, who refuse to retire and want to stay on for another crack even when the logic of life renders that impossible.

Spurred by his affection for Ligachev, Paloson proposed him in July for the Soviet Communist Party's number two position. Paloson thought it would be a good idea for Gorbachev to have someone at his side who could stand up to him, but Ligachev suffered a humiliating defeat, which forced him to retire from the political arena. Gorbachev, the great reformer, summoned the nerve to reject Ligachev publicly; they had been allies in the early days of perestroika, when the energy and desire for change had been the common driving force behind leaders who, in the end, were to go in different directions.

Paloson had not yet realized that society and the party had irrevocably split asunder, that consensus among the different factions in the Communist ranks was impossible, and that Gorbachev's arduous juggling act had collapsed. For Ligachev there were only his memories now. Not so for Paloson, who had one last battle to fight. His enemy was market economy, which was destroying his lifelong beliefs and might in the end split up his sovkhoz into private plots. He made ready to defend his position and also to mount an offensive.

A perfect product of the Communist system, Rembert Paloson was formed by that system's violence. He was born in Estonia in 1932, a citizen of an independent state, and spent his first years in the old university city of Tartu, where his lawyer father had a government post and his mother was a schoolteacher. The family lived in the schoolhouse. Russian was a foreign language to Rembert, although his mother, who had lived in Estonia when it was part of the tsar's empire, spoke it well.

The Nazi-Soviet Pact of 1939 and the annexation of Estonia by the Soviet Union changed Rembert's life. The last time he saw his father was the day before the man was taken away at dawn without the chance to say good-bye. Later the family was told that he had died in 1944. In fact, he had been shot in 1942 in a concentration camp near Sverdlovsk, in the Urals, but Paloson did not discover this until the late 1980s, when he was informed of the truth and received his father's certificate of rehabilitation.

Had his father suffered the same fate as the men whose corpses were disinterred in Kolpashevo by the erosive force of the Ob and dragged downstream to a point not far from the idyllic spot where Paloson now lives? These bodies, buried by the Stalinists in a mass grave back in the thirties, appeared in the water one day in 1979. A barge captain was ordered to chop up the bodies with his propeller and to keep his mouth shut. Such was the custom in that Siberian paradise where Ligachev was building socialism.

A few months after his father's arrest, Rembert, his mother, and a sister two years younger than he were deported by rail to Siberia. Packed like sardines, half starved, terrified, and exhausted, they made the journey of more than two thousand miles to Tomsk in a closed cattle car.

Paloson has never forgotten a moment of it, but when he was given the certificate of rehabilitation he made up his mind to accept the past. All that suffering can now be talked about openly, but not without pain. Paloson would rather describe the hospitality of the Russian peasants of Tomsk, who shared with him and his family "their last crust of bread" and saved their lives. He says it was his mother who taught him not to nurse any bitterness. She used to come in from the fields with calloused hands and never had the chance to be a teacher again.

Paloson learned to separate guilty individuals—namely, Stalin and his henchmen—from the system. "Who'd have thought, after what I went through, that I'd end up the head of the sovkhoz where I once plowed with a pair of horses? Who'd have thought I'd get where I have? It never crossed my mind, walking behind the plow and later driving a tractor, that I'd reach the top and even receive the country's highest decoration, Hero of Socialist Labor."

Paloson is proud of his ascent, of having achieved a position in a system in which, when he first arrived in Tomsk, he had had virtually no prospects. Rembert Elmarovich is tall and well built; his hair is silvery and his eyes blue. As a young man he must have been good-looking and caused havoc among the various Siberian girls he flirted with after his day's work. He married a local woman and brought up a family that tied him firmly to Siberia and Russia.

When his mother and his sister were allowed back to Estonia in the Nikita Khrushchev era, Rembert stayed on in Tomsk. "Estonia is my homeland, but Siberia is, too. I've spent my whole life there, all my working years," said Paloson. His children, an army officer and a teacher, do not think as he does, for, although they were both born and brought up in Siberia, their internal passports—which double as identity cards—record them as Estonians. This label may one day prove more useful than an identification as Russian.

On his lapel Paloson wears the Hero of Socialist Labor star that he was awarded in 1986. He won it for increasing the yield of his sovkhoz, which specialized in dairy products. His Estonian background helped, as he got advice from friends in the Baltic republics who were heads of kolkhozy and sovkhozy. He did not think, however, that the Baltic's privately run farms, small plots in the hands of individuals, would work in Siberia. There men had to protect themselves from the elements, towns were large, and there was a tradition of collective farming that did not exist in the Baltic.

Paloson, the "Soviet man," was not always blindly faithful to the system. From time to time he had opposed it out of sheer common sense. As well as its heroic dissidents, who suffered imprisonment, Soviet society had less exalted rebels. Their style was to work within the system and, where minor decisions were concerned, put forward the voice of reason. Paloson was one of them. "There were times when I could not carry out the orders I was given, times when I just listened and then did things my own way," he dares admit now.

A number of years ago, he recalled, as a result of a poor fodder crop, Ligachev decided to build a central feed store in Tomsk. The party committee, which at the time set farm policy in the region, worked out its usual cost analyses and decided to eliminate the sovkhozy and kolkhozy's small pig farms, which they found were more expensive to operate than a centralized unit. But Paloson had made up his mind to fight the decision, and fight it he did. The local party apparat mobilized. It called a meeting of the *raikom*, or party district committee, to which the *obkom*, or party regional committee, sent a special officer from their agricultural section to condemn the comrade's defiance in refusing to close down his sovkhoz's pig farms.

Paloson's voice assumed heroic tones. "They criticized me, they admonished me, they threatened me. They told me that if I didn't get rid of the pig farms they wouldn't give me state fodder. I held out, although I had to slaughter part of the herd. A year went by, and the *obkom*, headed by Ligachev, changed its mind. Events had proved it wrong. Official policy was reversed. The sovkhozy could have pig farms again. Yegor Ligachev called a meeting of the *obkom* and invited all the district committees to listen to the radio broadcast of the proceedings."

To Paloson's joy, Ligachev found that the decision made the year before had been "hasty." He told the gathering that "there were leaders who took the easy path and slaughtered their hogs, but there were also leaders who acted with foresight and, despite everything, hung on to the pig farms, among them Comrade Paloson." Thus had Ligachev commended the farms—only three in number—that had saved their hogs from the regional committee's arbitrary decision, made on his orders.

Paloson drew political conclusions from his small triumph. "Yegor Kuzmich," he said, referring to Ligachev, "recognized our right to think and act creatively." According to Paloson, the art of doing what one believed right, despite orders to the contrary, consisted in "knowing how to engage the people's support. With them behind me, I found it easier to act. In this case, the whole sovkhoz was in favor of keeping the pigs."

While we were talking in the heart of the Kremlin, a bumper grain harvest lay rotting in the fields for lack of transportation, storage facilities, and the labor to bring it in. I asked if this was not ample proof of the failure of the Soviet system of planning, which was unable to reap the benefits of nature's bounty.

Paloson thought that in some of the country's best grain-producing areas there was obstruction and even sabotage. If not, how was it that a country that exported oil had no fuel for its own farm machinery? The party and the state had abandoned their function as distributors. But why, when there were such shortages? Paloson believed that some hidden force was taking advantage of the instability and unrest. He contrasted the kolkhozy and sovkhozy system with Western-style farm consortia. The difference, he said, was that the kolkhozy and sovkhozy had never enjoyed independence, freedom, or means. He disagreed with those who likened Soviet farming to a bottomless pit that swallowed up vast sums of public money.

Now and again, the Soviet state had to absorb the losses of unprofitable sovkhozy and kolkhozy, subsidizing them in the name of an ideology that put collective ownership on a pedestal. The state would do anything rather than dismantle this system. It had written off Paloson's past debts, too, but they were from a long time ago, before he launched his own perestroika and began to introduce changes in the sovkhoz in line with ideas he had gleaned from his Estonian friends.

Paloson was not opposed to private farmers. In fact, he was quite ready to help them, but only "to supplement the sovkhoz, not to replace it. If we were to hand over our cows to privately run farms, the animals would not maintain their productivity, because it would be hard for a private farm to provide the well-balanced kind of feed that we can."

In his view, farm reforms should accommodate both large units and individual holdings. He was firmly convinced that in either case the state should retain ownership of the land, renting it out but not selling it. To sell land would cause a social upheaval and once again divide people into rich and poor. Paloson marshaled arguments against private property. Wealth and poverty in the Soviet Union would evolve for different reasons from those that brought about social inequality in the West. As a result of private property, the rich here would be people who had violated society's ethics, so anyone who did not break the law would inevitably be condemned to poverty.

Any present member of a kolkhoz or sovkhoz who had worked honestly all his or her life, Paloson argued, would never have savings enough to buy a piece of land. Only someone dealing in the black market, someone with a lot of money of dubious origin, could buy land and hire workers. Moreover, as Paloson saw it, people had not been brought up to deal with private ownership.

"I can accept private ownership of the means of production, but not of the land. Our people must not be divided. Private ownership of Russian soil will lead to chaos. The poor will become poorer, and the rich, richer."

Paloson would have liked a national referendum on the question of a transition to a market economy, but with or without such a vote he was now sure the shift would happen anyway. "At heart, I'm resigned to it," he suddenly confessed. "Not only personally but where my job is concerned. I'm already planning what I'll do when a market economy comes about and who I'll go into business with." Later on, before he left the Kremlin's Palace of Congresses, he said, "I think I'll manage."

I saw Paloson again in Tomsk at the end of September. I was the first Western journalist to travel to that city, which, owing to its importance in the defense industry, had been cut off from the outside world. Very near Tomsk is "Tomsk 7," a city that does not appear on any maps, Soviet or otherwise. Here, for decades, enriched fuel for nuclear reactors was produced.

The megalomania of the Soviet system, with its efforts to outdo whatever preceded it, has had a relatively benign effect on the character of Tomsk. The soul of Russia is still evident in the little wooden houses, especially those with the traditional carved window frames, and in the red-brick mansions built by merchants at the end of the last century. Tomsk was a major trading center on the route from Siberia to Europe before the town was overtaken by Novosibirsk, which was more conveniently situated on the Trans-Siberian Railway.

Like me, Paloson was staying at the October, a hotel that belonged to the Communist party and was by far the best in the city. He had driven the 150 or so miles from Kolomenskie Grivy to attend a Communist party regional conference. He was beaming with satisfaction: the harvest was in, and all preparations had been made for the coming winter. He had even managed to get a good half-mile of road covered with asphalt in exchange for a truck. Next year, for two more trucks, he would get another mile or so surfaced.

Paloson was growing more and more used to the idea of the free market, and the prospect of turning his sovkhoz into a company with shareholders seemed to him ever nearer and more intriguing. Even so, he was still unable to swallow any notion of private ownership of land. He was glad that Gorbachev wanted to hold a referendum on the subject, even though the outcome was uncertain.

We were talking in the hotel café. He proudly recited his farm's production figures. The Kolomenskie Grivy sovkhoz's forty-five thousand acres had triumphed again! Paloson praised Lenin and again declared himself a convinced socialist.

I wanted to know whether he sometimes felt a little let down, whether—now that things were changing so fast and socialism seemed to be finished—his life had been pointless.

No, he did not feel let down, nor was socialism finished. Socialism could and would rise again. For this reason, Paloson did not like the forces which, under the demagogic catchphrase of "perfecting socialism," were leading the country toward capitalism. He believed that other forces were on the march and that they would counter this trend.

As we said good-bye, this time outside the elevator, Paloson lowered his voice. It had been a good idea to talk in the café instead of in our rooms, he said. The old Communist made a sign of complicity and pointed to the walls. He was afraid of hidden microphones.

Moscow and Tomsk, September 1990

7

The Farmers of Smolensk

The province of Smolensk, on the western edge of Russia, has in its long history been a thoroughfare for invading armies. Its capital of the same name was founded in the ninth century and two hundred years later became the center of an independent principality. Since then, Smolensk has changed hands on a number of occasions, having been annexed by Lithuania and, later, by Poland. In 1812, it lay in the path of Napoleon's troops and in 1941, of Hitler's. With an area of nearly twenty thousand square miles, the province is a major industrial region, but its climate and soil are not favorable to farming. The Dnieper is Smolensk's chief river, and Yury Gagarin—the first man in space—is one of the province's most famous sons.

MIKHAIL Matsutsen gets out of bed before dawn, and the two cats asleep at his feet leap into the air, land together on the carpet, arch their backs, and pad off to the kitchen to launch into a new day of battle with the third cat, who commands a position high over the unlit old Russian stone stove.

The two cats that warmed Misha's feet came from Rostov with the Matsutsen family the previous spring. The third was left behind by the former owner of the house, a peasant who had worked on the local sovkhoz and who, the minute he retired, went to live in the nearest town. None of the cats has had a moment's peace. Amid the angry meowing that punctuates their skirmishes, they stake out their territory and tussle for control of the flimsy wooden cabin on which Mikhail has spent fifty-five hundred rubles.

Misha throws a few sticks into the room's second stove, a potbelly, which in gratitude immediately sends a wave of heat around the room where mother, father, and two sons sleep, a wardrobe separating their beds. The family prefers the potbelly to the *pechka*, the big Russian stove, which takes a long time to heat up. The *pechka* needs a babushka to keep it burning, and in the Matsutsen household there are no old people. The elder son helps out on the farm; the younger one still attends school.

Misha pulls on his quilted jacket over the sweater that his wife, Lena, has embroidered with his initials to distinguish it from the similar sweaters of their sons. He then slips out into the yard among the derelict rabbit hutches. Having no bathroom or indoor toilet is the worst of this life now that the cold weather has set in.

By the early light of the new day, Misha's eyes take in the landscape of run-down log cabins appearing amid the snow here in the heart of the province of Smolensk. Nearby lies the Moscow–Minsk highway, the main road connecting the capital with the western region, but civilization seems not to have penetrated beyond the front rank of pines and birches that flank the route.

Misha is a farmer. He's thirty-seven, slightly built, a grumbler, and a chatterbox. The adventure that brought him to this out-of-the-way spot began with a notice in a farming paper. One day, *Selskaya zhizn* (Rural Life) announced the start of a three-week course at Moscow University's School of Agriculture. Become an independent farmer in less than a month—that was the essence of the notice. The course was open to anyone, and at the end those who wished would be given land in the province of Smolensk.

Around thirty people, conspicuous in rustic caps and coats, signed up. All wanted to be farmers; not all had experience in rural life. But they had plenty of enthusiasm. Among them were Misha and two other would-be farmers, who are now his neighbors.

This was the first effort to encourage farming by individuals and was the brainchild of Nikolai Kharitonov, a professor of rural economy. Kharitonov's course taught the ABCs of subsistence farming in a program that smacked of survival training for prospective Robinson Crusoes. The students learned how much land must be kept in grass to feed how much livestock, which farm chores were crucial for basic survival, and which depended on the number of available hands in the family.

Kharitonov was trying to re-create a world that Soviet collective farming had destroyed at the end of the 1920s. It was not an exercise in nostalgia but a genuine attempt to restore man's bond with the earth, which in his view Communist agriculture had broken. At the end of the course, the professor wished his students luck and abandoned them like so many foundlings, sending them out to tracts he had somehow managed to wrest from the collective farms, which controlled all agricultural land in the Soviet Union.

A fierce advocate of subsistence farming, Kharitonov found it uphill work talking the directors of sovkhozy and presidents of kolkhozy into releasing uncultivated plots to future competitors. The heads of the collectives behaved like dogs in the manger. They were not using the land he asked for, nor did they want anyone else using it.

That spring, Misha and the other two farmers arrived in the hamlet with all their household goods. Given about 370 acres apiece, they settled in like exotic plants among the thirty or so families of elderly peasants retired from the local sovkhoz. The nearest village, Bogdanovshchina—with its school and two shops, one a grocery, the other selling general goods—is four miles away. Patient lines of old peasants wearing *valenki*, the felt boots typical of rural Russia, wait outside these shops. Neither Misha nor any of the other farmers own a car; they shop and take their children to school by tractor.

There is no bus service between the hamlet and Bogdanovshchina. The only link is Maria Timofeevna, who delivers the mail and, despite her sixty years, makes the journey on foot every day. For a modest sum, Maria Timofeevna will bring medicine or pension money to the housebound.

The presence of the farmers has split opinion among the hamlet's inhabitants—some are in favor, others against. Maria Timofeevna is one of those who supports the newcomers.

"They're young and hardworking," she says. "Let them be, otherwise the village will die. The rest of us are so old!" Since her daughter married a soldier and went off to Vladivostok, Maria has lived alone with her yapping dog.

Misha starts today, as he does every day, in the barn, where he keeps his twenty-five cows. The animals are on the thin side and give little milk, but for the time being they are his only source of income. The farm has cost him his life savings.

Matsutsen is wholly dependent on Kriukov, the local sovkhoz, which has given him the cows and the land. Misha does not own the land. He has been granted it "for life and with the right to bequeath it," but it is not his. Landownership is one of the Soviet Union's thorniest questions, and in the province of Smolensk the Communists, who are opposed to privatization, are a very strong group. The legal status of farmers like Misha is close to but not quite the same as private ownership. They are sailing a ship that has not weighed anchor.

Although laws are little more than useless paper in these unpredictable times, the current dithering over property ownership makes the farmers insecure. This uncertainty led Mikhail and Lena to hold a meeting in their house the night before to write a letter to President Gorbachev against a proposed referendum on private ownership of the land.

"We the undersigned farmers," the letter stated,

> are deeply concerned about the decision, taken by the Fourth Congress of Peoples' Deputies, which has trampled on our hopes and desires to own our own land. We believed what you said in the Twenty-eighth Congress of the Soviet Communist Party. We left our comfortable homes and came to the province of Smolensk to become farmers. We do not want anyone to make decisions for us. In our names and in those of our children, we ask to be given back the land of our forefathers.

Lena wrote the text out on a sheet of graph paper. The farmers decided to omit the words "left our comfortable homes," and they signed the letter. In point of fact, the referendum does not overly trouble any of the farmers, and still less Nikolai Gorokhov, head of the Kriukov sovkhoz, who has his own plans for updating farm management and is a black sheep among the lords of Soviet agriculture.

"With or without referenda, history does not march backwards. Events are already on the move. Who wants to go back to sovkhozy and kolkhozy?" said Gorokhov, who, along with the mayor of Bogdanovshchina and Professor Kharitonov, took part in the Matsutsens' nocturnal conspiracy.

On the same night, the farmers also sent a telegram of support to Boris Yeltsin and another to Ivan Silaev, the Russian government leader who was promising ten billion rubles to encourage private farming in the republic.

All those who met at the Matsutsens' house want to be rid of parasitical bureaucrats, who control access to credit and the distribution of fertilizer, land, and farm machinery. These officials head up an agricultural-industrial complex—the *agrokombinat*—which exercises its tyranny over the hamlet, the town of Bogdanovshchina, the Kriukov sovkhoz, and seventeen other sovkhozy. Kharitonov has spoken to the bureaucrats about projects for German investment in Russian agriculture, but they are apprehensive about any scheme involving private farms and fear rivalry from the farmers.

This autumn, as usual, the Bogdanovshchina school sent its children potato picking on the sovkhoz. But this time there was a difference. The farmers did not want their children taking part in the collective's harvest. If the children had to pick potatoes, they said, let them pick those in their own fields.

Misha has given up everything for farming. He once worked on a kolkhoz, and the experience left its mark on him. He had been unlucky. During the late Yury Andropov's law-and-order campaign, Misha was sentenced to two years' probation for fraud. He insists that he was only trying to get spare parts for the car belonging to the president of the kolkhoz, who gave him a free hand to follow his own initiative. In the end, the watchdogs of Soviet public property exposed Misha's operation, which involved trading watermelons, bottles of vodka, and plastic greenhouse sheeting for spare parts. Misha felt betrayed when no one would stand up for him, not even his boss, who had let him fudge the accounts.

"I'll never go back to a kolkhoz. Not even if they prohibit private farming. Never again," said Misha, who prefers the freedom of a pioneer's life to the slavery of the kolkhoz or sovkhoz.

The farmers and their wives spent the summer haymaking and sowing by hand, just like farmers of old. The worn-out tractor lent by the Kriukov sovkhoz does little to lighten their toil. In two years' time they have to deliver eight tons of meat to the sovkhoz in payment for the twenty-five cows. The sovkhoz buys milk from Misha and his friends at thirty-six kopecks a liter and sells it to the dairy products factory at seventy-two kopecks.

Anyway, the milk ensures the subsistence of the three families, even though some of the cows are no bigger than goats. The farmers have stopped milking the poorest of these, which suffer from rickets. If Misha and the others could, they would tell Gorokhov to milk the cows himself and they would go to a cattle auction and buy good stock—but they can't. In the next few days they will slaughter one toothless animal, the very one that eats the most and gives the least milk. They will share part of the meat and sell the rest to their neighbors. By night, secretly, Misha administers a dose of vitamins to the calves, hoping this will make them stronger than their mothers.

The farmers' worst problem is lack of credit. "I've asked the bank for a loan, but they won't give me one," says Misha. "They don't take us farmers seriously." Without credit, he and the others are condemned to live in the remote past. Without credit, they are dependent on charity from Gorokhov's sovkhoz, which in its turn is dependent on the *agrokombinat*, which takes the sovkhoz to task for frittering away the collective's resources by giving land to farmers.

The sovkhoz has trouble enough obtaining its own machinery

and spare parts, so it only gives the farmers what it does not need, which is little and not much good. They are all linked in the same chain of dependency. Misha would like to rid himself of his cows, and Gorokhov of the sovkhoz's many drunken scroungers. But scroungers do not want land, even if it were handed to them on a plate. Gorokhov is of the opinion that a little unemployment out here in the boondocks would soon wake up the idlers.

Misha is putting all his energy into his farm. He works from sunrise to sunset and never has a penny to his name. Despite this, when old Vanya, Misha's nearest neighbor, comes visiting one morning, he calls Misha a landowner. Vanya, whom the farmers have dubbed Old Birch, is a notorious grouch who lives with his son Alyosha, a retarded deaf-mute.

When the farmers moved in, Vanya lost the communal pastureland where he grazed his three sheep. This may explain why relations between him and the farmers are not unlike those among Misha's cats.

Old Vanya cannot accept the farmers. He sees them as a denial of all his principles, of everything he has ever learned. Vanya has rosy memories of the old days, when peasant brigades stopped work to sing, dance, and drink to the strains of an accordion. Work on the sovkhoz, he thinks, was happier than it is now on these private farms. In the past everything was clear-cut. He had been taught that landowners and kulaks exploited others for their labor.

In addition to Alyosha, Vanya has two other sons. One is in prison, a lost soul, and the other has gone to live in a city. Alyosha, who is thirty, lies on a bunk near the stove. He is asleep. From under the blankets a large shaven skull peeps out; Alyosha's eyes open, and he stares vacantly, his mouth gaping. On a stool beside him are some slices of bread and butter laid out by Vanya. Alyosha used to attend a special center. His father explains that the boy has something in his brain which makes him walk crabwise. He is docile and gives no trouble.

The old man is sixty-four but looks a lot older. His clothes are patched. Since his wife's death two years earlier, as a sign of mourning he has neither smoked nor drunk, but this has not stopped him from thinking about the future. He has been in touch with a marriage bureau, which has supplied him with several names and addresses, but they are all too far away from the hamlet. He wants nothing to do with any of the local lonely old women, of whom there are several. He would prefer a stranger, whose past he knows nothing about.

Vanya's house is full of dust. In its main room, by a potbelly stove, are his bunk and those that the rest of his family once occupied. He has piled several loaves of bread in one corner. These are provisions for him, Alyosha, the two piglets he has just bought, and the three sheep that no longer go out to graze. Every time Vanya thinks about the sheep and his lost pasture he works himself up into a rage and arches his back exactly like the cat left behind in Misha's house. The farmers laugh at him.

"Listen, old-timer, you can't even look after your garden and you complain we've taken your pasture away from you," Misha chides him, playing a chord or two on Vanya's accordion. "Graze your sheep there if you want. It's all right with me."

"I don't like this going back to the old ways. I'm used to Soviet rule," says Vanya, implying that the farmers are a throwback to the prerevolutionary world of landowners and masters.

"We're starting from scratch. We're worse off than you, and you call us landowners. It'd take us a hundred years to be landowners," says Misha.

The old man has a wardrobe full of trousers that Misha calls "a sartorial history of the Soviet Union." Vanya remembers the exact date he bought each item. Many are new, with price tags still on them. Some of the trousers were bought in 1958, during the Khrushchev era, others in Brezhnev's time, and yet others shortly before the particular style went out of fashion. Vanya has no good suit but he does have a new woolen one for being buried in. That way no one will have to worry about his corpse.

"It's tough having no wife," says the old man. "I have to

cook, wash clothes. My wife was everything to me. Look, wasn't she pretty?" He shows the only photograph he has of her, a thin peasant woman wearing a head scarf, and Misha drags out a melancholy note on the accordion. "Her name was Yevdokiya Vasilievna. We were married in 1951."

Vanya complains about shortages and blames the empty shops on Gorbachev. "You can't buy a thing any more. No candy, no cakes, no trousers. Look at the patches on these," he says, indicating the ones he has on.

"Time was when if I'd thought vodka would go up to ten rubles, I'd have gone crazy. Now ten rubles means a hundred. Money's worthless—just paper that won't buy anything. It all started with Gorbachev. Under Stalin life was hard. We paid a lot of taxes and had to hand over our milk, eggs, and cattle. The best times were under Khrushchev. Then, when he began doing foolish things, they got rid of him without any need for congresses of thousands the way they do now. They stopped Nikita, and everything went fine again. Things were good under Brezhnev, too."

Vasya and Maria, Misha's other neighbors, do not share Old Birch's opinions. Vasya is also retired from the sovkhoz. Were he twenty years younger, he says without the slightest hesitation, he too would have become a farmer. Vasya has the long beard of an old-time Russian peasant. As he does not smoke, he gives his cigarette coupons to Misha. He is glad the farmers are here. He thinks that the shops will fill up again, that if he and his wife fall sick or cannot gather firewood they will get help.

Vasya and Maria have four children, all of whom have gone to live in Moscow. "One stupid child's better than four clever ones," says Maria, referring to the company Old Birch receives from his son.

Even so, Maria realizes that the hamlet is no place for young people. The only fun the local boys have is visiting the weekend video club in Bogdanovshchina and flirting with girls who come to spend the summer with their grandparents.

Maria is a patient woman and understands Vasya's little excesses. His head muddled by vodka, he does not manage to reach the end of the patriotic poem that he insisted on reciting to us.

Misha and Vasya get on well. More than neighbors, they are cronies. They often get drunk together. And sometimes, like today, they look out on the snowy fields and begin to cry.

Bogdanovshchina, 26 December 1990

8

The Oil Poor

The Autonomous Territory of the Khanty and the Mansi, in western Siberia, endures long, hard winters and is part taiga and part tundra. Deep below the surface of its swamps and lakes are Russia's largest deposits of gas and oil. In addition to its oil industry, which began in the mid-1960s, the region produces timber and animal furs. The area's ancestral peoples, the Khanty and the Mansi, are reindeer herders and hunters of Finno-Ugric origin, who are now a minority in their own land. Their age-old nomadic life upset by the recent oil colonization, they have been forced to take refuge in the more remote and inaccessible parts of their territory. Surgut, a port on the river Ob, was a town of 7,000 in 1959. Today the lure of "black gold" has turned it into a city of over 248,000 people.

THIS morning, old Mikhail Vitaliev could not get his fur trap out of the river. The trap had been swept downstream, and he no longer has the strength to retrieve it.

The old man cannot row his boat anymore or keep track of his reindeer. During the summer, the herd is whittled down both by poachers and by the fact that a number of the more inquisitive animals stray into pools of oil that petroleum geologists leave behind in the taiga. Mikhail had over two hundred reindeer. Only when the cold sets in and the herd no longer roams free, browsing on the wild berries that fill the swampy woods in the brief northern summer, will he be able to tell how many reindeer he has left.

This summer it is not only the herd that has suffered. The old man's buckets and pots and pans have been stolen from his *izbushka*, as well as the skins he stores there for winter use. The *izbushka* is a kind of shed-cum-larder built on stilts to keep animals out. Mikhail blames the thefts on the parties of geologists surveying farther north on the border between the ancestral hunting grounds of the Khanty and the Nentsy. The two communities belong to what Soviet ethnographers call "the small peoples of the north." These are the twenty-six tribes, each relatively few in number, of indigenous inhabitants of Siberia. Here, in bygone days, the bear was held sacred.

The geologists—who are the precursors of oilmen, drilling rigs, heavy machinery, and pipelines—are old Mikhail's natural enemies. Like his ancestors in the district around Tianovskoe, he is a trapper, fisherman, and seminomadic herdsman.

Mikhail lives in one of the Soviet Union's richest regions, the Autonomous Territory of the Khanty and the Mansi, a dependency of the vast province of Tyumen, in western Siberia. The Khanty and Mansi territory itself contains over two hundred thousand square miles and a population of two million. The Khanty, however, are a minority numbering barely twenty thousand in all of Tyumen.

In winter, the boggy land where Mikhail lives turns into a solid layer of ice; in summer the forest is carpeted in thick mosses and swarms with mosquitoes. Deep within these swamps is a much-coveted sea of oil.

Thanks to its exploitation of places like this, the Soviet Union was able to pay its way as a military superpower and support a horde of parasitical bureaucrats as well as an extravagant, irrational regime. Over 65 percent of Soviet black gold is pumped from the Tyumen fields and more than 80 percent of the USSR's foreign exchange derives from oil.

The western Siberian fields were the nation's El Dorado. They, more than anything else, underpinned Soviet imperialism, for it was with this cheap oil during the deadly stagnation of the Brezhnev era that the USSR bought its allies' loyalty and complicity.

Back in the 1960s, when commercial exploitation of the Tyumen oil deposits began, the men who came from far away with their excavating equipment and their visions of wealth rounded up the Khanty and pushed them north. A similar plight had already befallen various Native American tribes in the United States. The difference here in the Autonomous Territory of the Khanty and the Mansi is that everyone involved has turned out a loser—the ancient peoples of the Ob and Irtysh rivers as well as those who came in search of oil.

Old Mikhail, the son of a shaman killed in one of Stalin's purges, is as abjectly poor as the ground on which he lives is immensely rich. Everything he has accumulated in his seventy years is in his yurt, a domed tent fashioned out of skins, bark, and bits of plastic stretched over a framework of branches. For most of his nomadic life Mikhail has been putting up and taking down this yurt, which accompanies him everywhere on a wooden sledge.

Although he understands Russian, Mikhail cannot or does not want to speak it. The Khanty tongue, in which he chatters away eagerly, has harmonies and rhythms reminiscent of Finnish and Estonian. The elderly man is small and agile and has no family of his own. He wears a leather jacket, and a dagger sheathed in reindeer skin is stuck in his belt. His companion, an aging Khanty woman, her hair in two wispy braids, shuffles aimlessly among the pots and pans. Her mind confused, she stares vacantly and never says a word.

The crone's two adolescent grandchildren, a boy and a girl, spend the summer in the yurt. Today they have gone to visit their nearest neighbors, twelve miles away. The children's father is in prison for killing his wife, the old woman's daughter.

Apart from Mikhail's hunting gun and the skins that serve as bedding, poverty is lord and master of the yurt. A few other possessions are littered about—dirty rags, spoons smeared with berry syrup, stale bread, a tea caddy, and a package of sugar. Outside the yurt is a black dog that never stops barking and a reindeer that cannot stand up. It lies beside the embers of a fire and gazes at the old woman with imploring eyes, its damp muzzle inhaling the smoke. One day, when lassoing the animal, Mikhail drew the noose too tightly around its stomach. "It won't live much longer," he says. Nearby lies the skeleton of another reindeer, with bits of fur still on it.

I flew in to this spot along the river Tromegan, sixty miles north of Ruskinskaya, in an Aeroflot freight helicopter. With me were Iosif Sopochin, president of the settlement's executive committee, and a midwife who doubled as an emergency doctor. Our expedition set off after rumors reached Ruskinskaya that Mikhail had fallen while fishing and broken a bone that had been fractured once before. So the helicopter crew had been alerted. In the vast reaches of Siberia, without roads or rail lines, Aeroflot helicopters are the main—and often the only—form of communication.

The helicopter lands us in a clearing and heads off north, carrying potatoes and other supplies to the geologists. Mikhail comes from the river to meet us. The news of his accident had been a false alarm, but the old man complains of eczema, which covers most of his body. The doctor smears an ointment on his arms and bandages them, while the old man smokes with great relish the cigarette I gave him. His slight frame does not have an ounce of fat on it.

His eyes very black and mustache very bushy, Sopochin talks seriously to Mikhail in the Khanty tongue and reaches a decision. In a few days, Sopochin will return to take the old man to Ruskinskaya. Where he will be lodged, Sopochin does not know. The hostel for nomadic herdsmen is not yet finished. Of the Khanty herdsmen in the Ruskinskaya census and under Sopochin's charge, a dozen are not strong enough to spend the coming winter in the taiga.

Ruskinskaya itself is not the best place to spend a winter, either. The settlement, a godforsaken place, sprang up in the 1930s, when the official policy was to force the Khanty to abandon their nomadic ways and take to the settled life of the kolkhozy and sovkhozy. Mikhail's life has not been untouched by the great events that have shaken the Soviet Union. For a while he looked after a collective's reindeer herd. His brother, like other Khanty, fought in World War II; their shaman father, accused of practicing witchcraft, was shot.

Located eighty or so miles north of Surgut, the main urban center in the Autonomous Territory of the Khanty and the Mansi, the town of Ruskinskaya is a monument to the uneasy coexistence between an ancient people in the process of being uprooted from their traditional way of life and newcomers attracted by the oil boom. The settlement has thirteen hundred people on its books, eight hundred of whom are Khanty. Of these, most are nomads, like Mikhail, and they spend their time grazing their herds in the taiga. Now and again they come to town for provisions or to sell skins and berries. Sometimes they trade furs to the geologists for vodka. As the Khanty do not know how to gauge their tolerance of alcohol, they invariably get very drunk.

An undulating dirt track wends its way through a landscape of lakes and woods, linking Ruskinskaya to Surgut and the outside world. At various points along the road, sandy islands have been created in the swamp, ready for a storage depot or drilling rig or cement works. The track stops short at the dunes that hide the town, a chaotic sprawl of log cabins and prefabricated huts. The oilmen have made an agreement to pave the streets, build a school, and expand the municipal central heating plant. But the streets do not exist, the school is not ready, and the heating is insufficient to warm the unfinished hostel for elderly herders.

The oilmen and geologists, who come to the settlement with a fever for black gold, are sent out from Moscow by institutions whose long names the Soviets are fond of shortening into acronyms. These oil monsters have little interest in Ruskinskaya. Their demands intimidate town and village councils, and when the oil overlords condescend to give anything to a community it is out of charity rather than justice.

What positive contribution have the oil fields made to the region? I ask Sopochin, who, at the age of thirty-seven, is conscious of his cultural identity as a Khanty. "Positive? I don't know what to answer. We might have progressed in another way. We've paid too high a price for civilization." And the negative? "They have destroyed our land and us as a people," he replies without hesitation. "Wherever they pump, it's on our soil."

Sopochin embodies a new awareness among his people. This has prompted the leaders of the Autonomous Territory of the Khanty and the Mansi to declare sovereignty over its resources. It has also prompted leaders in Tyumen, the regional capital, to freeze the bank account of one oil company for failing to fulfill its obligations in the area. All the constituent parts of the USSR are seeking the identity they lost under the unifying mold of "sovietness"; the territory of the Khanty and the Mansi is no exception.

Sopochin spent his early childhood in the taiga in a yurt like Mikhail's, "but cleaner." Later, while his parents roamed with their herd, he studied at a boarding school in a village near Ruskinskaya. He was six when he saw the first surveyors; the geologists came next. The whole conquest was a gradual affair.

Sopochin also talks in the melodious Khanty language at home to his wife. She is a teacher and is compiling a manual for teaching Khanty. The language is divided into a number of dialects so different that their speakers barely understand one another. The Sopochins' children speak but do not write Khanty.

Tianovskoe, where Mikhail lives, is the Khanty's last stronghold, but not perhaps for much longer. The geologists have found rich deposits there, and drilling is about to start. This summer Ruskinskaya's moving spirits, Sopochin and Aleksandr Krivykh, have fired off telegrams and letters of protest, and they have prevented oilmen from going ahead with their work. Krivykh is president of the local soviet, which is to say he is the mayor. Although a Russian, he has made the Khanty cause his own by virtue of his marriage to a local woman, a nurse, with whom he has three children.

The oilmen's arrival has changed life in the region. Heavy

machinery chokes the streams, blocking the migratory routes of the fish and killing them, and the reindeer are poisoned by the water. Krivykh unfolds a map dotted with hundreds of numbers that indicate present and projected wells.

"Work has started, and if it continues the people will issue the oilmen an ultimatum," says Sopochin. "I don't say it will come to a shooting match, but we'll give them warning. Last year, we drove off the geophysicists." He tells me this to show that there's a fundamental change of attitude among the Khanty, a fighting mood that did not exist before. "Our people are very peaceable," he adds. "That's why we've been so easy to oppress."

Oil exploration in western Siberia, long dominated by greed, is inseparable from the name of Gennady Bogomyakov, former First Secretary of the Communist Party of the province of Tyumen. Embodying the will of the system, he battled to raise Tyumen production to a million tons a day. At that time, the oil gushed spontaneously out of the ground and had only to be piped. Later, the wells lost their pressure and needed pumping. Production costs rose, but Moscow's thirst was insatiable.

Both the Khanty and the newcomers on the lookout for easy money were caught—and are still stuck—in the same trap. The former have seen their magic world vanish without having been given another in return, and the "conquerors" have seen their dream of riches disappear the same way. Years of squalid living in makeshift shacks or even in gasoline tank trailers have left them embittered.

Valentina and Roman Nishitin are as poor as old Mikhail. They are from Novocherkassk, and live in a barrack hut in Surgut. Roman, a crane operator, came here eight years ago. His wife, Valentina, a hairdresser, joined him three years later. They have been on a list for a house ever since they arrived. Their present quarters consist of two rooms so narrow that in one of them their bed and their daughter's touch.

The Nishitins' rooms are as untidy as Mikhail's yurt. In the room in which they eat are a table covered with an oilcloth, shelves for dishes, and hangers holding suits and dresses that will not fit in the wardrobe. Large Ukrainian headscarves drape the clothing. Valentina cooks on an electric stove in the passageway, and the smell of fish fills her house and seeps into the one across the way, where the couple's neighbor Vyacheslav Gordeev lives. Gordeev, who is from Volgograd, earns six hundred rubles a month, and he estimates that if his firm built ten apartments a year, he might get one in sixty years. In Gordeev's house, a single room also with two beds, the chaos is even greater than in Roman and Valentina's.

Roman and Vyacheslav are watching television cartoons together. Both men are bare-chested and wear sweatpants. Both hold flyswatters that they wield skillfully against the treacherous Siberian mosquitoes. The men's movements, slow and rhythmic, have the look of a new sort of dance, an absurd, grotesque dance of nagging poverty.

What is the oil doing for Tyumen? What is it doing for the men who bring it out of the ground or for the people whose traditional way of life has been destroyed? Over a period of several days, I put these questions to senior administrative and financial officials in Surgut and Tyumen.

The replies take various forms, but the content is always the same: nobody around here is getting so much as a crumb. The banquet is being gobbled up far, far away. Oil production is a good example of how the centralized Soviet system functions. Tyumen pumps crude oil but loses control over it the moment it enters the pipeline. Lacking refineries, the region then has to bring gasoline for its cars back in from other parts of the country.

The political stopcocks are also outside the province. Tyumen had no reason to support the government's decision to cut off oil to Lithuania when it was struggling to establish its independence. In fact, Tyumen had more cause to oppose the blockade, since, in exchange for oil, brigades of Baltic workers had built whole towns in the region. Better organized than their Russian counterparts, the Balts completed work on schedule.

Before 1990 the oil agencies were treated, for all intents and purposes, as if they were industries in need of subsidy. Their targets and budgets were determined in Moscow, but they never saw a kopeck of the profits. This arrangement ultimately created such a scandal that in 1990 the agencies were authorized to retain 5 percent of their foreign exchange earnings on crude oil exports. With the dollars wrested from the ministries, the oil agencies kept their workers happy with handouts of Danish sausages, underwear, and Japanese video recorders.

"We'd have been better off not knowing about all this wealth of ours. The standard of living in this country is one of the lowest in the world. We should have thought less about World Revolution and more about the earth we live on," Vladimir Kozyr, a Russian parliamentary deputy, tells me in Surgut. "Once upon a time we thought our destiny lay in the labor of our hands. We thought that by working harder we could improve our lives. Things turned out differently. However hard we worked, we couldn't rise above a certain level. When we realized this, it was terrible."

Kozyr, who left the party after the Twenty-eighth Congress, now belongs to the Parliamentary Group of Workers and Peasants, a heterogeneous alliance that also includes Aleksandr Bir, the miners' leader from Novokuznetsk. Placing more faith in Yeltsin than in Gorbachev, Kozyr thinks the former is going forward from the point where the latter left off.

In 1985, when Gorbachev visited Tyumen, Kozyr "sang his praises"; in 1987, he "loved him"; today, in 1990, he merely respects him. Something ties Gorbachev to the old system, the deputy believes, and this prevents him from being completely honest with himself. He is anchored in the past along with the cruiser *Aurora*.

Tianovskoe, Surgut, and Tyumen, August 1990

9

———————————■———————————

Fear of Power

The city of Novokuznetsk, located on the banks of the Tom in the Kuzbas coalfields of western Siberia, is a product of Soviet industrialization and Stalinist forced labor camps. From 1932 to 1961, the city was called Stalinsk. Now the center of Siberia's steel industry, Novokuznetsk fuels its towering furnaces with coal from the area's rich deposits. Dreary, polluted towns that offer their inhabitants few comforts have sprung up around these mines. Novokuznetsk, more than two thousand miles due east of Moscow, is also an important rail center. Its population of six hundred thousand makes it the largest city in the province of Kemerovo.

THEY offered us power, but we didn't know what to do with it," recalls Aleksandr Bir, an organizer of the 1989 miners' strike in the Siberian region of Kuzbas. A year later, he sees those heady July days—which at the time appeared destined to change his coal-mining life forever—as a military campaign that ended in stalemate.

At the crucial moment, an army of hundreds of thousands of angry, dirty, hungry men demonstrated to the world their faith in Gorbachev and their fear of responsibility. Made dizzy by the power within their grasp, they themselves put on the brakes. Bir, one of the strategists of the workers' movement in the Soviet Union, feels that at this juncture a historic opportunity vanished into the polluted skies of Novokuznetsk, Kemerovo, Prokopievsk, and Mezhdurechensk, the cities that during the strike gave their names to the battles won in a war that was lost.

Bir cites the Bolsheviks, who in 1917 did not shrink from responsibility. They knew how to use and to direct the workers. Riding the crest of a wave of social protest, the Bolsheviks saw how to harness this raw power. But the Kuzbas miners and the Bolsheviks were two different groups.

"Over the centuries we Russians have grown used to a patriarchal form of rule," says Aleksandr. "We've always trusted someone from above to provide for us. In other countries, individuals rely on themselves for their welfare. But we've always had God or a tsar. We're used to handouts. Communist promises of a rosy future have only encouraged our lack of initiative."

In the 1990 elections, the miners' leaders used the popularity they had acquired during the strikes of the previous summer to get themselves elected as deputies to the Russian Parliament and to regional and municipal soviets. Bir became a deputy to the Supreme Soviet of the Russian Federation. Now, as a member of its Legislative Committee, he is engaged in helping to reform the penal system. In this connection, he spends a lot of time making the rounds of the country's prisons. The work has given him contacts with the police and security forces.

Bir dislikes the limelight. He prefers to remain in the background, where he can act as a facilitator and bring other people to the fore. I met him through the economist Vasily Selyunin, who got to know Bir while touring the Russian coalfields. Taking his cue from events in Poland, Selyunin was trying to establish some sort of common ground between intellectuals and workers. Normally the two had little to say to each other. According to one view, the intellectuals lived off the sweat of the workers, who distrusted them. Moscow intellectuals, moreover, knew next to nothing about life in provincial Russia.

Bir and I have talked on a number of occasions: in the Kremlin, during Russian parliamentary sessions; at the Rossia Hotel, where he stays when he is in Moscow; and in Novokuznetsk, where we spent a day together shortly after the first anniversary of the strikes. The current of anticommunism, which one sensed beneath the surface in 1989, erupted into the open in 1990. One after another, the Kuzbas mines have held meetings and evicted the Communist party from premises it had been enjoying at the various pitheads.

Born in 1942, Bir has not had an easy life. His Soviet-German parents were interned by the Communists when Hitler invaded Russia in 1941. His mother died in a labor camp, and his father remained in captivity until 1954. Bir grew up in a Novosibirsk orphanage, where he was placed as an infant. At the age of thirteen, he started working. Recently, in an old, faded photograph, he saw his mother's face for the first time, and it was her resemblance to his daughter that convinced Bir the face was indeed his mother's.

Aleksandr believes in discipline, reliability, and long-range undertakings, by which he means the step-by-step development of a movement to protect workers' interests both now and in the future. In his view, the 1989 strike has not ended but has only been "interrupted."

The independent workers' movement grew out of the Kuzbas strikes. From there its influence spread to miners in Vorkuta, on the Arctic circle, and to those in the Donbas region of the Ukraine. The grass roots of the movement were the strike committees—later known as workers' committees—organized in the mines and in city and regional councils. The Workers' Confederation, a nationwide coordinating body along the lines of Poland's Solidarity, was founded in the spring of 1990. Unlike Solidarity, however, the Soviet workers had no intention of making political involvement their primary aim—and they said so.

All over the country in the early years of perestroika there were short, spontaneous, isolated work stoppages that received scant notice in the media. People in the West, dazzled by Gorbachev, knew next to nothing about the dismal lives of Soviet workers and peasants. The Kuzbas strike escalated popular protest to heights that astonished even those who, like Bir, had laid the groundwork.

"In 1988 we got together on a number of occasions, looking for ways to express our dissatisfaction," he recalls. "We didn't know whether to call a meeting or issue a statement." At these gatherings, the last thing the Kuzbas workers had in mind was a strike, even when they noted how low their living standard was compared with that in Moscow. Nor did strike action in the coal mines of Sakhalin, on the Pacific coast, or Karaganda, in Kazakhstan, or, to a lesser extent, locally seem to provide a precedent.

Bir is thin, with fine features. His eyes have the thoughtful look of an intelligent, self-educated man. When he speaks, he reveals a mouth full of gold fillings. "Hours had increased and wages had been reduced," he says. "I was earning less than I had at the end of the 1960s, even though I was now an experienced face worker."

In Kuzbas there were reasons to fear what Bir calls "a critical situation." The region had more prisons and reformatories than anywhere else in the country. For years, former inmates had been obliged to settle there after serving their sentence. "In Novokuznetsk, one in five of the population has been in jail," he continues. "The potential in this for trouble worried us."

Events were getting out of hand. The shops were empty, but Bir suspects that the shortages, which included food and soap, might have been staged. "There were elements interested in provoking social unrest," he says darkly. "They wanted people to come out into the streets and start looting. With so many ex-convicts about, Kuzbas was a perfect place for sparking off an uprising."

At the beginning of July, Bir went back to work after recovering from an accident in which he lost three fingers of his left hand. In the interim, mine workers at a pit called Shevyakov, in Mezhdurechensk, had drawn up a modest list of grievances and warned that if by 10 July their demands were not met they would strike.

No one took the ultimatum seriously until the appointed

night, when the miners refused to go down into the pit. From then on, the strike spread like wildfire. In their working clothes and helmets, the men marched defiantly through the city streets and picketed the local Communist party headquarters.

On the eleventh, a municipal strike committee was organized in Mezhdurechensk. Bir attended as an observer. He was anxious to stem any outbreaks of violence, especially those of fellow miners. Having assumed responsibility for public order, the miners had quickly prohibited the sale of alcoholic beverages anywhere near the pits.

The police provided an escort. At first Bir thought they were trying to encircle the strikers but he soon realized he was mistaken. The police, seeing the uselessness of opposing the miners, had instead taken their side.

The spread of the strike forced the coal minister, Mikhail Shchadov, to come to Kuzbas. Shchadov rushed from one place to another like a man trying to put out a grass fire. He would arrive at one place, talk to the miners, accept their demands, and think he had solved the problem. But the problem, which was the same wherever he went, kept cropping up, each time in the form of a new and larger list of grievances.

Bir, too, moved from place to place along with the strike; he hardly slept; he helped draw up the strikers' demands; and he coordinated the committees, formed first in the southern cities of the region and then in the north. By 14 July the miners' demands were everyone's demands. Steel, chemical, construction, and transport workers all wanted to join the strike.

"To tell the truth," Bir recalls, "the breadth and dynamism of the movement scared us, and we made the others go to work. If we hadn't put on the brakes, two of the country's biggest steel mills would have struck. This would have paralyzed transportation and brought society to a standstill. When the minister read the list of demands, he clutched his head and said most of them were beyond his scope. The miners told him, 'If you can't do anything, speak to the government or get an authorized representative sent out here.' In a state of shock, Shchadov wired Moscow. Hang on a while, the Politburo told him, and they would send a special commission.

"It was at this point that we made a conscious decision. We would not lay down any political demands that we didn't have the muscle to back up. We still had faith in Gorbachev. In both his domestic and foreign policy I saw him as our most responsible statesman. By doing what we did I thought we were supporting him."

Basic loyalty to the system and to Gorbachev explains the bad treatment the miners handed out to activists of the Democratic Union, the only opposition political organization at the time that could have made effective use of the workers' movement. The Democratic Union offered its services, but the miners rejected them. "Just to have said yes to them would have been enough," says Aleksandr.

On 19 July, as a result of negotiations with the special commission sent from Moscow, an agreement between the government and the miners was announced in Prokopievsk. At these negotiations, instead of taking the miners' side, Stepan Shalaev, the smarmy leader of the official unions, had supported the government. There was nothing unusual about this. In many industries it was difficult to convince official union leaders that their job was to represent the workers, not hobble them.

Combining statements of principle with details as specific as the delivery of fifteen hundred square yards of carpet to the region, the Prokopievsk agreement was an ingenuous document. Bir, however, likened it to a treaty between nations.

"As the result of a bloodless revolution," he claims, "a whole region had been put in the hands of strike committees. If at that moment we'd had real political power behind us, we could have created a new state in Kuzbas. They gave us the power, but we didn't know what to do with it. We were too few. All we were thinking about was the money side."

Having calmed the atmosphere, the government and the min-

ers drew up a full document in Moscow. It was called Protocol
608. Bir immediately began to wonder how the government
would go about fulfilling all of Protocol 608's utopian promises.
Whose share of the pie would be taken away to give to the
miners? Bir compared the government to a tailor who tries to
make a suit by cutting up the trousers to make the jacket, except
that in this case there was material for neither. Moreover, the
miners had to tolerate the fact that their comrades from the other
industrial sectors—whom the miners had dissuaded from strik-
ing—now called the coal workers "privileged" for having
grabbed crumbs that were not theirs.

Bir's dream of a workers' movement has secret roots. Membership in the Communist party from 1971 to 1988 had given
him long experience of bureaucrats who pretended to represent
workers before the latter began to speak for themselves. He left
the party when he saw that its structure was unable to serve his
ends.

"I used to think that fighting from within the party was the
only way to achieve my ideals. But one day I saw that I had to
destroy the party itself," he recalls. Bir believes that in the past,
during what is now known as the period of stagnation, there
was a chance to stand up for the workers from within, and in
spite of, the system. "You had to develop your own methods,
you had to know how to pull strings and at the same time cover
yourself so you wouldn't be accused of antisocial or antistate
activities. Anything that fell outside the existing framework was
dangerous."

Back in the seventies, in an act of complicity that Bir's fellow
workers all felt but could not openly express, they elected him a
member of his mine's union committee. That position gave Bir
legitimacy. In those days, to protect the workers' interests might
simply mean refusing to accept higher productivity targets. Since
no one for decades had bothered to modernize the mine's tools,
machinery, or technology, the only way to show the steady rise
in productivity that the system demanded was to extract more

work from the miners. Thus manpower became the system's most malleable element.

To emerge unscathed from a whole series of conflicts of this sort, which flared up throughout the seventies, a particular sort of skill was required. Bir knew the rules of the game.

"I had to avoid direct confrontation with the government and keep out of politics," he says. The miners could threaten "not to go down the pit" (Bir had done this on one occasion), but to breathe the word "strike" was taboo. "I was a Communist. It was the only way to look after the workers' interests without getting into trouble. I could not have done what I did any other way. Someone had to point out the defects of the system. People like me, Communists who could be used as examples, were necessary. Leaders could get up in public and say, 'Meet Comrade So-and-so, a Communist who's making a stand.'"

Such Communists, however, could be tolerated only if they remained local, isolated phenomena. "I could mobilize a section of my mine," Bir says, "but had I tried to mobilize the whole mine I would have been branded a dangerous individual. So I had to be very careful."

In the mid-1970s Aleksandr's eyes were first opened to the outside world when by chance the Russian version of a German mining journal fell into his hands. It allowed him to compare the two countries' living standards, wage levels, accident rates, life expectancy, and coal production figures. The reality around Bir seemed backward and primitive. He subscribed to the journal and gradually began to mature.

But it was a long time before he understood that "the bite of one mosquito out in the provinces" was not only never going to change anything but would make things worse. At best it would lead the authorities to give to some what they took from others less outspoken or weaker. This was true both of the mines and of the country at large. It was the key to the balancing act of Soviet society.

The hostility that Bir began to feel toward the system was a classic worker's reaction. He saw that bureaucrats had kept workers and peasants from governing the country. Bir meant "real workers" and not the "lackeys" rewarded for their loyalty to the regime—"heroes of Labor so busy presiding over ceremonies they have no time to work. The regime stuffs them until they no longer remember what hunger is and it makes them think they've won medals for real merit. They don't realize they've been fattened and pampered so that they can be shown off on public platforms, where they shout, 'Long live the party! Long live the working class!'"

In 1988, as a mark of protest at the undue influence of apparatchiks in certain of the party's internal elections, Bir resigned, an act then viewed as "treachery." Today Aleksandr's greatest fear is that he might fail to measure up in the eyes of his comrades. They expect too much, he thinks. They want their leaders to be heroes and they also want change in the twinkling of an eye.

"I'm afraid it will be five years before we can bring about real change," says Bir. "We're so far behind that all we're doing now is scattering seeds that may bear fruit in ten or fifteen years' time. If we can't keep the promises we make, we'll come to grief just as the party did. People won't give us their votes, and we'll be denied the chance to put our beliefs into practice."

Voters ask Bir what Boris Yeltsin would give them. "Nothing, I tell them. We must radically change our outlook. We must fight for ourselves. It's not a matter of anyone giving us anything, it's a question of not sitting back and waiting for a handout."

Chaos is Aleksandr's worst nightmare. It would have a domino effect that would proceed to shake the West and endanger the whole world. Should this happen, "only a strong figure could save us, someone not afraid of blood or of spilling blood, someone who could steer society onto a governable course, stay in power long enough to create order, and then retire from the scene. When a society falls apart, it's no time for ethics. What's needed is a person who knows how to use power. He will restore order and prevent the country from going under. If there's a choice between infamy and disaster, I for one am ready to choose the former, even if history reviles me. If a Malyuta Skuratov* is necessary, so be it."

Novokuznetsk and Moscow, July–September 1990

---

*Skuratov, the sixteenth-century figure who headed Ivan the Terrible's secret police, is associated in the Russian mind with ruthless repression.

10

―――――■―――――

The *Partkoms* Must Go!

S PEWED from the chimneys of factories all over the city, among
them the gigantic steel mills with thirty thousand employees,
smoke and dirt hang in the thick air. Sweating men and women
line up in the street under a torrid summer sun to buy ground
meat. The vendor, a woman in a neat white coat, weighs out
scoops of the fatty mass that she takes from a metal tub on the
sidewalk. Although covered by a big white napkin, the tub is
swarming with flies.

It is lunch hour in Novokuznetsk. I pass the makeshift meat
stall, its smells mingling with all the other street smells, on my
way to talk to leaders of the Kuzbas workers' movement. Our
meeting is to take place in the local House of Political Education,
a headquarters for the propagation of party doctrine. Such buildings are found in every provincial city of any standing all over
the Soviet Union. Here, in a borrowed room, the Novokuznetsk
Workers' Committee—the group that originated in July 1989 as
the Novokuznetsk Strike Committee—has set up an office.

The Kuzbas workers' movement is the best organized group
of its kind in the country. Nowhere else in the Soviet Union does
the movement represent so many sectors of industry or have such
an influence on local decision making. In Kuzbas the workers'
committees make up a sort of shadow cabinet, and without their
say-so nothing can be accomplished.

The Novokuznetsk Workers' Committee consists of miners
elected and paid by their own co-workers. The committee's job

is to oversee the implementation of agreements made with the government in 1989. Since the miners' movement first erupted, more than a year has gone by. During that time, the committee has come to the bitter realization that miracles do not happen.

"The government has played with us as if we were children," says Viktor Agoskov, one of the four "liberated" mine workers who is on duty here this morning. ("Liberated" is the term used for those paid to serve on the workers' committee instead of performing their usual jobs.) On a wall is a sign inviting activists to leave the party. "Help a comrade get out," the notice reads. It sounds like a plea to give up a vice, such as drug addiction.

Of the "liberated" four—Viktor Morozov, Viktor Agoskov, Igor Feskovich, and Mikhail Deinekov—only the last still belongs to the party and even he, a member since 1979, is about to resign. "I see no future in it," Deinekov says. "I delayed my decision to leave until the Twenty-eighth Congress, hoping there'd be some radical changes. The Communist party does not represent the working class. There's no political force today looking after workers' interests. Nor is there any other party on the horizon. There's nothing but the workers' movement itself."

As we talk amid a cloud of cigarette smoke, the conversation leaps back and forth between mutually exclusive ideas: state ownership versus financial independence for the mines; the Communist party versus the workers' movement; the Soviet Union versus the Russian Federal Republic; Gorbachev versus Yeltsin. In the end, these antitheses boil down to one stark conclusion: "Our system is completely unworkable."

"Rampant socialism is to blame," says Agoskov. Never active in the party, he is, in fact, against all parties. "This system is finished. Everyone knows it. Gorbachev knows it, the Politburo knows it, the Communists know it, but they all just sit there when what they should be doing is getting the hell out."

To get the hell out. This is exactly what the workers of Kuzbas are demanding of the party officials ensconced at the top of the big industries. "The *partkoms* must go!" is the new watchword. *Partkom* stands for party committee, an institution which, like the *profkom,* or union committee, has had a cozy niche in every Soviet factory, mine, and collective. In Kuzbas, the workers' assemblies are getting rid of the *partkoms,* throwing the members out of their offices along with all their ideological kitsch: imitation marble busts of Lenin, political works that no one reads, and out-of-date slogans, like those that still adorn the facades of some of the city's buildings but no longer command anyone's attention.

The vacuum left by the *partkom* and its officials, whose salaries came from party dues, is now being filled by workers' committees. Such is the aversion to bureaucracy that members of the Novokuznetsk Workers' Committee have chosen to become unpaid officials of their new movement. Each month they have to justify their existence to the group at large, which is free to demote them and send them back down into the mines.

This morning Vladimir Kolesnikov has traveled to the committee's office from Kemerovo, the regional capital. He is "liberated" and a member of the Democratic Union, the first political group since perestroika to call itself a party. The Democratic Union was always rabidly anti-Communist. When the strikes began in 1989, its few members in Kemerovo were more or less under wraps. Their new magazine, *Svobodny Kuzbas* (Free Kuzbas), has just been published, and it contains the addresses of eight representatives from all over the region.

Kolesnikov, with his fair hair and bushy beard, has the air of a man opening up some vast new territory for development. He has come to establish a branch of his party in Novokuznetsk, where there are ten or so active members and a number of small internal problems. He passes around copies of *Svobodny Kuzbas,* describing to the others the fight to open a newspaper stand in Kemerovo for selling "informal literature." This designation applies to papers and magazines that do not have government approval and therefore receive no state subsidy. Kolesnikov tells them about Mikhail Batugin, an active member of the Democratic Union who had been trying to run the newsstand. When the Ministry of the Interior confiscated Batugin's stock of "informal literature," he had responded by going on a hunger strike. Only after the material had been returned to him did he call off his protest.

This afternoon members of the Democratic Union from Badaevskaya mine plan to hold a meeting. "Do you want to come?" Viktor Morozov asks me. At fifty-three, he is proud of never having been a Communist, although—according to him—they tried to recruit him many times.

"I deliberately did not join the Communist party," he says. "I don't like its ideology, and I've too often seen the way the head of the *partkom* would dictate to the mine manager exactly what he should do."

Even though the *partkom* was officially responsible for ideology, in practice it also involved itself in economic affairs. Now that ideology has been smashed and the party no longer interferes in financial matters, the *partkom* has lost all reason to exist. This is a logical result of the establishment of democracy and the move toward a market economy.

Badaevskaya mine has a work force of 2,300, with 372 Communist party members, 170 of whom are retired. As in other mines in the region, the exodus from active party membership has accelerated. In 1989 there were just over 50 resignations, but in the first seven months of 1990 the number had already risen to 130.

The Communists assemble in the mine's Palace of Culture, with its gilded plaster moldings. Aleksandr Varyonov, the *partkom* secretary, announces that he has made up his mind to go with the tide of history and abide by the decision reached at workers' meetings held a few days earlier that called for the removal of *partkoms* from the mines. This leaves the *partkom* members demoralized and insecure, as if they had been orphaned, for they do not know how to function outside the mine, which they will now have to do.

The bitter fight over the four rooms occupied by the *partkom* in the mine offices is a small-scale reflection of the greater struggle to expel the party from the country's political leadership. The best option for the Communists would be to relocate *partkom* offices in party headquarters. Some see in this strategy the party's last-ditch hope for a revival of Soviet-style communism.

The Communists are still in disagreement among themselves, but what is clear is that nothing will be the same as before. These days, he who takes the bit between his teeth gets his own way. A few hours after the meeting in the Palace of Culture, Lyubov Kazakova decides to blank out the sign "Party Committee" on the office door. She covers it with a sheet of white paper that looks a bit like a shroud. A little round woman who takes all these goings-on with a pinch of salt, Kazakova is about to return to teaching, the field she was "liberated" from fourteen years earlier to work on the mine's board of Political Education.

While Lyubov Kazakova laughs, Svetlana Svetlakova, editor of *Shakhtyor* (The Miner), sobs. She complains that she has no typewriter, no tape recorder, no office, no telephone even, to help her publish *Shakhtyor,* the erstwhile organ of Badaevskaya's *partkom* and *profkom. Shakhtyor* will probably cease as a party organ, and the motto "Workers of the world, unite!" will vanish from its masthead. More than likely, *Shakhtyor* will swell the ranks of the workers' movement press, whose best publication is the weekly *Nasha gazeta* (Our Paper). Although printed—not without conflict—on presses belonging to the Communist party regional committee, *Nasha gazeta* is virulently anti-Communist.

Svetlana is a little over forty and quite attractive. She wears lots of eye makeup and a thin summer dress that shows off her figure and gives the miners a bit of a thrill. Apologizing for her tears, Svetlana manages to use them as a female ploy, thereby eliciting a few patronizing words of sympathy from Varyonov. Both will end up drowning their sorrows in a bottle of vodka that we shall all drink later at Svetlana's house, together with Viktor, an Afghanistan veteran, who is number two in the mine's *partkom.*

Thanks to Afghanistan, Viktor now has a good car, bought "without standing in line," which means that he has had to compete with World War II veterans in "the line of those not in the line." Viktor has started a group in Novokuznetsk for former Afghanistan soldiers and found a job in the mine's store for Sergei, who lost an arm and an eye on his "international mission."

Badaevskaya mine is a microcosm of Soviet paternalism. It builds apartments for its employees and nurseries for their children; it runs a farm and even maintains beehives. Its head, Ivan Khazmin, barely has a minute for what should be his main job, the profitable extraction of coal.

"Social matters take up all my time," says Khazmin. "If only I could concentrate on the mine!" He is responsible for four nurseries; the Palace of Culture; a stadium; two central heating plants; a herd of 150 pigs; a grain silo whose contents are threatened by dampness; the farm, which is run-down; the hives, which are producing no honey; and the apartments, which, built at a rate of forty a year, will never adequately house his work force. Before 1989, the workers could expect to wait an average of thirteen years for a living space of eight square yards per person.

"I doubt whether the mine makes a profit. Nothing's been renewed in it for fifty years. Targets are imposed on us from above, and the one aim has been maximum production." Khazmin is forty-three; he arrives at the mine by five in the morning. He's been a party member since 1979. It is an unstated but obvious fact that he would not have been allowed to run the mine without previous service in the Communist party.

A new political awareness is awakening in Khazmin. He was a member of the mine's strike committee in 1989. In theory the strike was about pay, but the agitation had a clear political side to it. At the time, miners whispered to foreign correspondents that they were fed up with the party.

"Last year we managed to fend off political demands," says Khazmin. "Now, however, they're the order of the day. I myself have begun to think like our workers. I feel the government should resign."

What about Yeltsin? "He's gaining in authority, but let's see

where we stand in two more years." Khazmin so fears wide-
spread upheaval that, to avoid it, he would endure stern measures. He is also afraid of a power vacuum, on the grounds that
fascist groups may slip into the space vacated by the Communist
party.

The government has entitled coal mines that export to keep
15 percent of their revenues. Badaevskaya mine's foreign earnings are controlled by the Kuznetsugol consortium. However
much the Kuznetsugol tries to convince the miners otherwise,
they think the consortium is manipulating the figures. As if toss-
ing a bone to a dog, from time to time the consortium tosses the
miners a handful of imported consumer goods: televisions, sausages, clothes, and the occasional Japanese car, like the one the
manager drives.

On paper, Igor Gladun has obtained more autonomy for his
mine, Polosukhinskaya, than his colleague Ivan Khazmin has for
Badaevskaya. Since January 1990 Polosukhinskaya, with a work
force of nineteen hundred, has been "leased" to the miners. In
practice, however, the state is still laying down conditions, fixing
the price of coal—well below market price, according to Gladun—acting as go-between, and dictating how the mine must
use its revenues.

Over a loudspeaker system, Gladun, a small man, raps out
orders from his office. Following the party's Twenty-eighth Congress, he announced on a popular local television show that after
fifteen years of service he was thinking of leaving the party. If
the mine were his, Gladun would lay off a third of his work
force (administrative staff first of all), introduce a new pay scale,
and bring in modern technology and equipment. But what he
would most like is for his mine to be the first to attract foreign investment. "Of course, foreigners are all fearful of our
instability."

The autonomy of Polosukhinskaya today amounts to little
more than a "permit" to export two hundred thousand tons of
coal. In practice, only a quarter of this quantity seems likely to
get the necessary "license." A representative from the mine spent

two weeks tramping from one office to another among the Moscow ministries before he found someone in authority to secure the license. Now Gladun has to repeat the exercise to find an intermediary to ship the coal abroad. The path to financial independence is long and complicated.

Gladun fears that in their eagerness to find a scapegoat his comrades will end up cutting off innocent heads. The wave of approaching chaos could, he thinks, unseat Gorbachev. In Gladun's opinion, the Soviet president travels abroad too much, has not dealt forcefully enough with armed nationalists, and has shown little respect for the radical democrats.

Polosukhinskaya's manager claims that at the next strike he will join the workers in the streets and tell everyone loud and clear that he wants new leaders. "I don't want to get mixed up in politics," he points out. "But no matter what I do I can't seem to avoid it."

Novokuznetsk, July 1990

11

The Ax

The town of Novaya Derevnya, with its two thousand inhabitants, is about twelve miles from Moscow on the old road that leads to Sergiyevski Posad (formerly Zagorsk) and the Troitsko-Sergiyevskaya Lavra monastery, the spiritual seat of the Russian Orthodox Church. Sretenia, Father Aleksandr Men's parish church, is a wooden building that was brought to Novaya Derevnya in 1922 from a village about to be drowned by the damming of the Ucha River. In the past, when it figured as a stopping place for pilgrims, Novaya Derevnya was a country village where Muscovites could spend the summer within easy reach of the capital. Today it is part of the capital's urban sprawl.

J EWS don't usually like Dostoyevski. Check it and you'll find that few Jews keep Dostoyevski's books on their shelves," claimed a man from the Russian hinterland, who risked being misunderstood in voicing such a remark to a foreigner.

The man was trying to explain to me that Russian culture contains a symbolism inaccessible to anyone whose Soviet passport, in the space for nationality, bears the designation "Jewish." In his determination to make his point, he was saying what others feel but leave unspoken.

I wanted no part of a dirty secret that divided the world into two incompatible groups—those who love Dostoyevski and those who are unable to love Dostoyevski—but the man's words started me thinking.

That conversation took place a few days before my appointment with Father Aleksandr Men, who was both "Jewish" and a priest of the Russian Orthodox Church. The person I had spoken to and Father Men did not know each other.

At the time, Reverend Men was priest of a parish in Novaya Derevnya, on the outskirts of Moscow. His church was a small, clean wooden building set back from the road, as if to protect it from the stares of the curious, in a landscape that combined the remnants of a village with the industrial sprawl of the capital.

The faithful came in thousands from great distances to hear Father Aleksandr. In his sermons they sought ways to fill an emptiness, to dispel the desolation that was spreading over the length and breadth of Russia like a huge black cloud. Not only because there was no bread, soap, sugar, vodka, or tobacco, but also because life was devoid of meaning and the future, of hope.

It was Father Men's belief that what set humans apart from animals was the search for meaning in life. Father Aleksandr found this meaning in religion rather than in Marxist philosophy. He had grave reservations about Marx's view of the evolutionary nature of history. This view, he conceded, was an optimistic one, but the Bible, his favorite book, did not share it. Christianity's emphasis was on man's responsibility for working out his own salvation.

For most of the Soviet Union's citizens, who no longer wanted to be mere "comrades," it had been a summer of disenchantment. Not for Father Aleksandr, however, because he had a mission. "There are those who write history and those who live it out. I'm one of the latter," Father Aleksandr told me four days before his death. "The gospel is my life."

Father Aleksandr's portly figure, draped in a wide-sleeved, worn black cassock, moved with surprising agility and grace. He had twinkling eyes and a silvery beard, and was as ready to preach a sermon as to publish an article. He gave lectures, baptized the children of a leading intellectual, and held church weddings for couples who had had civil marriages. Putting on his tall black hat, which suited his face so well, he would administer the last rites to an elderly friend. Father Men could not stand idle. He was a missionary, and before him lay the huge task of gathering into the Christian fold as much of Russia as his tireless activity could embrace.

As an ecumenicist, Father Men recognized no frontiers. He operated from within the Russian Orthodox Church, but this institution was a point of departure, not a refuge from the world. His vast goal was to take the rigid world that the Russian people had inherited from Marxism-Leninism and fill it with universal culture. To do so, he had to revive subtleties, breathe fresh air into the areas that had been starved of it, dust off altars, and refurbish oratories. Father Men laid the bricks of this worldwide culture with the Bible in one hand.

"You must study the Bible. Not only does it permeate our civilization, inform the daily life of old Russia, and stand at the root of Western culture, but without the Bible you cannot understand Russian poetry," he was to tell his students at the Gorki Institute of Literature two days before an ax took his life.

The young literati listened to him avidly. Father Men did not believe that the wealth of the Bible lay in its historical relevance alone. Calm in his conviction, he stressed his disagreement with rationalist biblical scholars on this point. He saw dissent as an enriching force.

"Freedom is in the mind and can occupy a greater or lesser space," said Father Men. "If we had a device to measure freedom, each of us would register a different level." He went on to add, "Anyone who wants to grow spiritually must build a fortress inside himself."

It was early September, his first lecture of the academic year. One of the students, a young girl with a candid face, asked the priest if it was true that the Virgin Mary had recently appeared in Moscow and condemned Marina Tsvetaeva's poetry. Father Men was careful not to reply cuttingly. The Virgin, he said, had better things to do.

"Has Russia a mission?" asked a languid-looking young man. The priest thought for a moment. "Yes, it has. Russia is the crucible where East and West come together."

For the previous two years, since the KGB gave him the green light to do as he wished, Father Men had had a full schedule and had become a popular figure on the Moscow social circuit. Atheists and believers, the parameters of whose faith or lack of faith were blurred in the chaos typical of a period of transition, flocked to the Institute of Historical Archives and the Writers' Union club to listen to this man expound brilliantly in public what he had been saying fearlessly in private for nearly thirty years.

Son of the head of a textile factory, Father Men owed his Russian Orthodox upbringing and his secret baptism to his mother. At first, Aleksandr had not wanted to enter the seminary. He had started life as an apprentice furrier at a cynegetics institute in Moscow and later in Irkutsk, in Siberia. This allowed him to travel across the tundra and the taiga, in contact with nature, which he loved. It was at this time that he met Father Gleb Yakunin, with whom he shared a room for three years. A former political prisoner, Yakunin was now one of the most outspoken radical deputies in the Russian Parliament.

Father Men had often been asked to enter politics, but he always refused. He had no taste for it, but he could understand other priests embracing politics at a time when the country's stability depended on everybody's effort. For priests to join political parties, however, was unacceptable to Father Men.

How strange it must have felt for him to speak the name of the new organization he belonged to: The Bible Society of the Soviet Union. Suddenly, in conjunction, the words "Bible" and "Soviet Union" no longer sounded two discordant notes. And it had been a long time since the KGB had tried to drum up a charge that would take him to prison and out of circulation. They had had good cause in the sixties and seventies. There was the set of slides about the Bible that he himself had glued into frames to show to children; there were the books he had published abroad and those he distributed in the Soviet Union; there were the secret baptisms that he performed in private homes.

Yury Senokosov, a neighbor of mine, had known Father Men for years. Together they had published Russian philosophers who were officially banned. Yury, Aleksandr, and other friends

distributed books by Nikolai Berdyayev, Aleksandr Solzhenitsyn, Georgy Fedotov, Sergei Bulgakov, and Semyon Frank in
samizdat editions of thirty copies typed on onionskin paper by
a trusted and not overly expensive typist. Father Aleksandr had
copies made of everything that came into his hands, including
papal encyclicals and a Russian edition of *Camino,* by the Spanish priest Monsignor Escrivá de Balaguer, the founder of Opus
Dei, the elitist Roman Catholic organization of laymen and
priests.

In this way, as the little group of friends copied and distributed, the Brezhnev, Andropov, and Chernenko eras passed.
Those years were a cultural dark age. More than once, Father
Aleksandr had been called in for interrogation by the KGB. Now
that his library was free to circulate around Novaya Derevnya,
and his catechism groups for adults and children met openly,
Father Men bore no one a grudge. He even held that the KGB
had always been "very correct" with him. Those who were close
to him knew that the priest never talked openly about the anonymous threatening letters he received.

The crime pages in the Soviet press had once been full of
articles denouncing Father Men. "Our ideological enemies per-
sist in their attempts to incite and subvert the weaker elements
in society," announced the newspaper *Trud* (Labor) in a 1986
series of articles entitled "A Cross on the Conscience." "Those
who fall into our enemies' clutches are all too easily confused
and turned against our country."

Luckily, the atmosphere of liberalism heralded by Mikhail
Gorbachev prevented the noose from being tightened around
Father Men's neck. Gorbachev, according to Father Men, had
performed a seminal act when for the first time in the nation's
history he separated church and state. Paradoxically, the Russian
Orthodox Church had been more resistant to change than the
Soviet state.

The church, whose survival had been bought with its silence,
wavered over its own reform. For decades it had retreated into
the Middle Ages, holding fast to its Old Slavonic liturgy, its

offices that made up the canonical hours, and its austere fasts. The Orthodox church was remote from the man in the street, whose concerns were fixed on the present.

I had to wait for hours before I could see Father Men, who kept shuttling back and forth between the sacristy and the church. That day a Russian under secretary of education had come to ask the priest's advice. Father Men had also had to marry an old couple, who had been witnesses at another wedding and, after thirty-nine years of civil marriage, suddenly decided that they too wanted to be married in church.

For a whole year, while working in the parish of Novaya Derevnya, Father Men spent much of his time on the suburban train traveling to Moscow and returning to his house in Semkhoz, near the Zagorsk monastery. He had always used train journeys for writing. The religious books that were only now appearing in the Soviet Union under his real name had been composed back when he had been forced to publish abroad, under a pseudonym.

Father Men's assistants were discussing a nostalgic television program that equated Russia with the Orthodox church and the tsars. The program made the assumption that the burning down of churches and the assassination of Nicholas II were crimes the Russian people could not have committed wittingly; someone must have been behind these acts. Of course, that vague "someone" was the Jew, who could not love Dostoyevski.

"I don't watch that stuff. I can't stand it. I'm going to bed," said Father Men, bursting out of his office. The small room was full of books, and photos of his friends covered its walls. Here were Nadezhda Mandelstam, to whom he gave extreme unction; Aleksandr Galich, the singer-songwriter whom he baptized before Galich emigrated; and Solzhenitsyn, who had been a friend. Father Aleksandr believed that the reason Solzhenitsyn was undecided about returning to Russia was his cultural dilemma. With whom should he align himself, the liberals or the fascists?

Although he had not seen the television program, Father Men was worried about the resurgence of "Russian fascism." He was concerned about boys who, for a few rubles, peddled in the streets samizdat editions of the spurious anti-Semitic tract *Protocols of the Elders of Zion*. Worst of all in his view were certain street vendors who, before selling one of these pamphlets, asked the prospective customer, "Are you Russian, brother?" It was this behavior that had prompted Father Men to resort to his own samizdat to explain the origins of those texts, whose aim was to convince gullible Russians of the existence of a worldwide Jewish plot.

Father Men was sure that many clergymen actively supported fascism. "There's a direct link between Russian fascism, the Russian clergy, and nostalgia for the church. This is shameful to those of us, the believers, who look to the church for support. Instead, it's the fascists whom the church supports. Wherever you look in the church, you find monarchists, anti-Semites, and anti-ecumenicists."

Up until then, Father Men had scarcely been aware of any of these people. Where had they come from? Before 1975, Father Men claimed, he had never encountered anti-Semitism in the Russian Orthodox Church. Fifteen years later, it seemed to him that anti-Semitism was one of the church's "dominant traits."

"When Gorbachev opened the floodgates, out came democracy and, with it, a fascist backlash. That's what we have now, and a backlash is always violent," he noted. Anti-Semitism was a compensatory mechanism. "People need to blame someone else for society's offenses. Instead of Russians taking responsibility for the destruction of their churches, we make the Jews into sin incarnate. It's hard to admit this, but that's the way it has been. Russians bear the guilt for destroying thousands of churches, but they can't face this fact, so they look for a scapegoat. No one's ever punished for abusing Jews. Cowards always attack the helpless."

In Russia, Father Men pointed out, there had never been a de-Stalinization comparable to the German de-Nazification. To Russians, "patriotism" was still an acceptable word. No intellectual liked Stalin, yet ordinary people felt that in his day things were better. Father Men recognized that nationalism was an extreme reaction against a system that had tried to crush national differences. But he feared an ensuing "cultural narcissism" and the rise of new closed societies, especially in Roman Catholic republics like the Ukraine and Lithuania, which should have been in the forefront of ecumenism. "Only self-confident societies are strong enough to be open to others," he said.

Yesterday, Father Men came upon a young monk criticizing a parishioner for folding his hands in a non-Orthodox manner. This struck Father Men as a symptom of petty fears. "Peter the Great, a well-known agoraphobic, had all the rooms in his palace built on a small scale. In religion, as in life, there are those who suffer from neuroses."

I did not dare tell Father Men about Dostoyevski and the man from the Russian hinterland, but I did tell him about a priest I had met that summer in Tyumen. This gentle cleric, Father Mikhail, believed that the Russian Orthodox Church was full of Jews and Freemasons. A man of thirty-seven who had studied in Moscow, he was convinced that church circles in the capital were ridden with faddists and Zionists.

Beauty contests, pornography, and rock music frightened Father Mikhail, who was teaching his three children to read with a 1914 primer, which dated from before the reform of Russian spelling. Father Mikhail's friends also believed in the Jewish conspiracy. They did not like the new patriarch, Alexei II, because he was "part German, part Estonian, and part Jewish."

Father Mikhail's friends, members of the nationalist group Otechestvo (The Fatherland), believed God was on their side. They were firmly against ecumenism and condemned the inroads Catholicism had made into Orthodox thinking. They also claimed that the Orthodox church was tainted, and that all Russians were to some degree infected by Zionist values and were victims of secret Catholic propaganda. Father Mikhail's friends admired the Spanish Inquisition, which they viewed as a necessary evil for preserving the state.

"Unlike the Jews, who are only interested in profit, the Russians have a mission to save the whole world," I was told by a girl in Tyumen, who, in her devotion, sometimes got lost in mists peopled by phantoms. Her phantoms were called "Jews." She saw them everywhere—in Tyumen's petrochemical plants, which poisoned the air of Russians, in the top ranks of the state, and in the Communist party leadership.

She could tell a Jew from a Russian but could not explain how. By their names? No, Jews were always changing their names. By the shape of their faces or their physical appearance? Neither. The Soviet peoples were so interbred that Russians could no longer be distinguished by their physical features. By language? Everyone spoke Russian, but there were nuances that made some of the great writers in Russian into non-Russian writers. So how could she tell which were Jews? It was a question of sensibility. The pious girl admitted that although in theory a Jew could be part of Russian culture, in practice this was impossible.

"He's typical," said Reverend Men when I told him about my encounter with the Tyumen priest and his friends. "Your kind priest may never have met a Jew, but the Jew is his demon, the Moby Dick that he must slay."

That summer, men calling themselves priests of the Russian Orthodox Church, men who considered themselves "Russian writers," railed against ecumenism in the pages of magazines like *Nash sovremennik* (Our Contemporary) and *Molodaya gvardia* (The Young Guard). A monk named Georgy Fedotov claimed that "the teachings of the church categorically forbid Orthodox Christians to pray with heretics" and warned that "those who preach ecumenism are trying to unite everyone in one faith under the leadership of the Jewish synagogue."

Reverend Men was a Jew, but in his library were any number of books by Dostoyevski. He said that this author leads readers down the black corridors of hell, not so as to leave them in the depths but to bring them out on the other side.

The Ax

Father Men operated within a framework of Russian culture. Russian was his mother tongue: he preached in Russian, prayed in Russian, and died in a very Russian way. His death was worthy of Dostoyevski. He was killed by an ax blow early on the morning of 9 September 1990 as he was leaving his house near the Zagorsk monastery to catch the local train, which would have taken him to his parish. He was able to stand up and stagger a few steps, but the blow had been a powerful one, and Father Men's portly figure slumped down for the last time on the woodland path that led from his house to the station.

Father Men was fifty-five. Who struck the fatal blow or why, nobody knew. Once again Raskolnikov's ax—the ax, which, with the cross, is one of the symbols of the Russian world—had claimed a victim. We will never know how much missionary work was cut short by an ax wielded by someone who did not believe in ecumenism.

I could not help thinking about Dostoyevski and the man from the Russian hinterland as Father Men's body, in an open coffin according to Orthodox practice, was carried by pallbearers into what had been his parish church for a funeral that this time was his own.

"What can you say about a country that kills its apostles?" murmured a parishioner.

A few days later, a gentle monk overflowing with holiness refused the money he was offered to conduct a mass in memory of Aleksandr Men. The monk apologized. He had conscientious objections; he could not officiate at a mass for someone who had undermined the foundations of the Russian Orthodox Church.

Novaya Derevnya and Moscow, 5–7 September 1990

12

———————◼———————

A Soldier Mayor

Ryazan, an industrial center in the midst of a predominantly farming region, is located in European Russia, about one hundred miles southeast of Moscow, on the Oka River, a tributary of the Volga. The city's commercial concerns include a petrochemical complex, an oil refinery, an agricultural machinery manufacturing plant, and a food processing factory. Among Ryazan's many historical buildings are a fifteenth-century citadel, or kremlin, several seventeenth-century churches, and a monastery dating from the late seventeenth and early eighteenth century. It also has a museum that commemorates the physiologist Ivan Pavlov, a native son, who discovered the conditioned reflex. The city's current population is more than half a million.

THE Moscow–Orenburg mail train reaches Ryazan at dawn, taking almost four hours for a journey of little more than a hundred miles. The old town of Ryazan, whose history is steeped in feudal princes and Tartar hordes, is still asleep as I make my way from the station by the yellow glow of street lamps that barely light up the road. To reach my hotel, the Moscow, which neighbors the city hall, I pass row upon row of dilapidated old houses. In the Middle Ages, when what is now the nation's capital was an insignificant huddle of dwellings in the principality of Vladimir, Ryazan was already an important place.

Today, however, it is merely a provincial city with the problems of all Russian provincial cities, and emotions are running high between the old Communist oligarchy and the new partisans of change. The former are building up their strength within the regional party structure, while the latter close ranks around Mayor Valery Ryumin.

A statue of Lenin, disproportionately large for the buildings around it, dominates the main square. This is the town that gave the world Ivan Pavlov, the renowned professor of physiology and discoverer of the conditioned reflex. Commemorative plaques in his honor can be seen here and there on decaying mansions that once housed a snug nineteenth-century society. Like so many other Russian cities of its kind, Ryazan wakes from its nightly slumbers amid the ruins of its past. Its onion-domed kremlin, whose thick walls are in a perpetual state of restoration, rises dank and soulless above puddles formed by the thaw. Meanwhile, people line up at a newsstand to buy the local papers. The conservative *Priokskaya pravda* (Oka River Truth) lashes out against Mayor Ryumin's leadership. *Priokskaya pravda* is the organ of the local Communist party, and Leonid Khitrun, its head, is not on Ryumin's side.

Daily life in Ryazan is a struggle. Since the breakdown of the Socialist Common Market, when Hungarian-built Ikarus buses became too dear for the Soviets, public transportation vehicles have not been replaced. In the gray morning, trolleybuses carrying more people than they can comfortably hold leave jam-packed for Ryazan's industrial areas. More than 70 percent of the factories here are engaged in secret branches of the defense industry. Such activity does little to replenish the municipal coffers.

A sunflower-seed vendor has set up trade on the sidewalk at a trolleybus stop, her superfluous tidbits highlighting the general absence of bare essentials all over the city. Nearby in a bakery, customers prod the big round loaves of black bread and find them much too hard. The quality of Ryazan's food is such that were Pavlov to use it for his experiments today, the good professor's dog would scarcely move a muscle, let alone salivate. Typically, there is not even a café where one can shake off the sorry experience of the Hotel Moscow, with its communal bathrooms, drowsing watchmen, and constant stream of guests shuffling down the corridors bundled up in bathrobes.

I am in Ryazan to observe a day in the life of Mayor Valery Ryumin, who is kindly allowing me to sit in on his meetings throughout my stay.

"Deputies may enter without waiting in line even if the president is busy." This is the sign that Ryumin, as president of Ryazan's municipal soviet, had put up over the door of his office when he was elected mayor in 1990. Later, he pinned up beside the sign the text of the Declaration of Russia's Sovereignty, thereby proclaiming his own loyalty to the fledgling Russian state.

As well as being mayor, Ryumin is president of the Association of Russian Cities, and in his place of work, he has neither a bust of Lenin nor portraits of Mikhail Gorbachev, but he does have a small photo of Boris Yeltsin. From the photograph, Yeltsin looks at Ryumin, holding out his hands in a gesture of friendship.

At forty-one, Ryumin is an energetic, athletic man whose bearing recalls a military past. Once lieutenant colonel of a parachute regiment, although now retired, he still refers to himself as a soldier. His military training reveals itself both in his decisive movements and in his tone of voice, which can suddenly change from the informal to the peremptory. Signs of his past are also apparent in his work habits and constant vigilance. Ryumin is a man who boasts of having no secrets. Unobtrusively, I sit in on the many meetings the mayor holds in a long day that extends far into the night. A postmortem on the city architect's resignation, a meeting of municipal advisers, and a debate on the General Structure Plan form part of our program.

Lieutenant Colonel Ryumin came to Ryazan as a teacher of Marxism-Leninism at the Paratroop Academy. He had been decorated in Afghanistan, where he was wounded in an unsuccessful operation against the mujahedin. The Russians had suffered forty casualties in the action, among them six of Ryumin's companions. The senseless war affected him profoundly. The world he had believed in since childhood, when as a model student at Tomsk high school he had played war games with his schoolmates, had collapsed. The faith he had still held to when, as a nineteen-year-old cadet at the Novosibirsk Military Academy, he joined the Communist party, had been destroyed. Afghanistan changed something that even his reading of prohibited books by Leon Trotsky and Nikolai Bukharin in Moscow's Lenin Political-Military Academy had been unable to alter. Afghanistan opened Ryumin's eyes to what he had never once questioned in the barracks, where command of his troops left him no time to think or read.

Ryumin was stationed in Afghanistan from 1980 to 1982 as *zampolit* (second in command of the Political Section) of a paratroop division. He saw generals getting drunk and loading anything of value they could grab into military cargo planes. Only there in Afghanistan did he at last come to realize that he had been deceived and that *Pravda,* the newspaper he trusted, was not the Truth at all.

"Suddenly, I found out that *Pravda* was telling it all backwards. I was there, I saw what was going on, and the lies were an enormous blow to me. If *Pravda* was so obviously lying about whom we were fighting for in Afghanistan, then could we believe anything else it said?"

Sometime in 1981 Ryumin wrote a report on the outlook for the Soviet presence in Afghanistan. His paper, whose conclusion was that to have sent in troops had been a mistake all along and that to remain there now was pointless, was read at an officers' briefing and relayed to the general staff with the support of the major general. The report had no effect on either Ryumin's career or the course of the war.

Ryumin's wounds were moral as well as physical. This realization surfaced only later, during his Marxism-Leninism classes at the Paratroop Academy. He was so critical of the system that his superiors forbade him to teach or to speak to the cadets about politics. Ryumin, however, was not alone in his disenchantment.

Others were waking up, too, and in a city like Ryazan, which boasted four military academies and was the headquarters of a parachute division, it was hardly strange that when change came it was dressed in uniform.

In 1989, reform of the Soviet political system opened up new horizons for Lieutenant Colonel Ryumin. A group of civilians and cadets asked him to run for election to the Soviet Parliament. At first he refused, but little by little he relented. His full reversal came in response to the humiliation suffered by a colleague, who was preparing to stand for election when the directors of the academy forced him to withdraw his candidacy. Ryumin was not about to accept the fate of his fellow officer.

"Are you going to back down?" the cadets asked Ryumin. He did not, but his superiors at the academy were adamant about banning political activity by military personnel, and they did their utmost to prevent any gathering of the hundred persons required to propose a candidate. To thwart a possible late-night conspiracy, the commanders assigned an officer to sleep in each section.

"Despite all this," Ryumin recounts, "one night the cadets got out of bed and organized the feared electoral meeting. They collected more than five hundred signatures. Even so, the heads of the academy refused to accept this."

Ryumin's progress was brought to a violent halt on 5 April 1989. On that day, several hundred truncheon-wielding policemen broke up a group trying to hold an election meeting. Several participants were injured; others were arrested and fined. "People were furious. It was the first time anything like that had happened."

The incident backfired. In the elections for the Russian Parliament the following year, Ryumin—with the backing of thirty-two thousand signatures and the endorsement of numerous businesses—cleaned up at the ballot box. As well as winning a parliamentary seat, he was elected president of the municipal soviet of Ryazan. "The political wind had changed. Tricks used against independent candidates in previous elections angered people. In the municipal elections, not a single one of the old guard passed the test. Rejection of the Communist party was total."

The soviet that Ryumin inherited in the spring of 1990 was a poisoned gift. A soviet, the basic unit of Soviet parliamentary structure, is a large council and as such bears little resemblance to the kind of mayoral office that exists in the West. Until the shake-up that Gorbachev dealt the soviets, they were powerless, decorative edifices limited to rubber-stamping Communist party decisions. In the shadows behind the soviet and its executive committee (*ispolkom*) were the regional committee (*obkom*) and the municipal committee (*gorkom*) of the Communist party. The party made decisions, the soviet carried them out, and, if things went wrong, the latter was held responsible.

After Gorbachev's reforms, the soviets, claiming their historical mandate to exercise "all power," not only defied the party but began to appropriate arbitrary legislative and executive powers. Scrambling for areas of jurisdiction previously denied them, some soviets went so far as to declare sovereignty over their own air space. Others established import and export restrictions, and still others allowed the registration on a local level of exotic political parties. One such was the Party of Islamic Revival, which came into being in a neighborhood of Moscow. During all this activity, Ryazan remained somewhat backward. Nobody here even knew how the civic structure worked.

As soon as he became president of the soviet, Ryumin recognized that a body of 175 deputies was too unwieldy, even though the democrats among them were in the majority over a Communist minority of 73, headed by one of the local KGB chiefs. To take control of executive power, Ryumin assumed the presidency of the *ispolkom*, replacing this body with a group of advisers consisting of professionals from the various sectors of the municipal economy, such as factory directors, public transportation heads, and so forth. After the Twenty-eighth Congress, Ryumin left the party. He now complains that the Communists are making his life impossible by spreading lies about him.

"They claim that I bought a foreign car for two hundred

thousand rubles, that I got one hundred thousand rubles for my parents' house, that my wife found me in bed with another woman and set fire to the bedroom door, that all this summer I've been the only person in the city to have hot water. They say the most absurd things. I pay no attention. This is a pitched battle, but we knew what we were getting into. It came as no surprise when the party tried to sling mud at us."

Ryumin stays on his toes. Army friends keep him posted on the climate of opinion within the military. In September 1990, when conservatives and democrats were accusing each other of planning a coup, an unexpected movement of troops toward Moscow worried the mayor. On 9 September, the Ryazan parachute division was put on alert. Even soldiers on leave were urgently recalled. Armed to the teeth, they were transferred to Moscow. There they were told that "unofficial movements"— the term in the period before Gorbachev's reforms for any opposition group outside the recognized political organizations— were proposing to overthrow the government. The troops were given civilian clothes so that they could infiltrate any demonstrations, and they also mounted guard around the generals' dachas on the edge of the capital.

Almost at the same time, on the night of the tenth, two parachute regiments in the city of Pskov were put on alert. The soldiers were divided into two groups. The first was taken to Tushino airport, in Moscow, and the second landed at Ryazan airport without having notified municipal authorities of their intention.

When the reformers demanded an explanation for all this military activity, the Soviet Defense Minister, Marshal Dimitry Yazov, said that the soldiers were rehearsing for the 7 November parade in Red Square. This response did not satisfy the reformers. Having visions of a military coup, they kept their eyes open. Ryumin helped them from his front-line position in Ryazan.

The mayor's chief aide was Sergei Voblenko, a professor in the Academy of the Ministry of the Interior. There were also the twenty-two members of the Ryazan soviet who were soldiers.

The mayor's relations with KGB officials, however, left much to be desired. Ryumin accused them of trying to discredit him on the eve of the elections by spreading the rumor that he was four parachute jumps short of the number required to qualify for an army pension.

In its day-to-day affairs, the new reformist council of Ryazan is often overwhelmed by a sense of impotence. For instance, when the opposition won the elections, the immediate reaction of the Communist party municipal committee was to dissolve and take with it the files of the city's Socioeconomic Section, which contain data about factories and other commercial enterprises. It was as if it had absconded with the medical history of a patient about to undergo a tricky operation. The new city council found itself suspended in midair. An enormous effort was required to reassemble the most basic data, even simply the number of existing companies. To this day, the soviet has not reconstructed all the Communist party's links with local industry; in the meantime, the defense industries—while trying to move away from armaments—still deal with the party regional committee and ignore the city council.

"It's early yet to expect them to cooperate," says Ryumin. "I think we should let them suffer a bit longer; then they'll come around."

Although the Communist party has formally withdrawn from municipal life, it continues to function through the regional and neighborhood committees, which are a thorn in the flesh of the city council. The Communists, in fact, dominate the Ryazan regional soviet, which has prevented the city from carrying out plans for physical expansion. On the one hand, the party boycotts the General Structure Plan that sets out to determine the city limits; on the other, it refuses to give the city land because there is no approved General Structure Plan.

To Ryumin, the problem is not that the general plan is out of date and does not take into account the privatization or liberalization of businesses. What he wants is for an actual area to be delimited as urban rather than rural. In Ryazan, almost all municipal services belong to the regional soviet. These range from barbershops, grocery stores, and bakeries to taxis, buses, and the local radio and television studios. (These last have put a ban on both Ryumin and any discussion of private farming.) The city's trolleybuses, which operate at a loss, and the kolkhoz market remain in the hands of the municipal soviet. Having managed to snatch the market away from the regional soviet, Ryumin has promised refrigerators, televisions, and cars to peasants who bring meat to Ryazan.

"We want people to see that a municipal soviet exists—a municipal soviet that has taken over the market and does not follow the party line," says Ryumin.

Ryazan is broke. The city budget depends on regional funds, which take 90 percent of local taxes. The city receives only the crumbs, the least lucrative taxes. It cannot build houses, renovate the municipal heating plant, or upgrade the urban sewage system. Previously, regional leaders helped resolve these problems. Now they hold back, and potential suppliers of materials are asking to be paid in kind—that is, with fuel from the local oil refinery. This fuel, like everything else of value in Ryazan, does not belong to the city council.

In these times of transition, old schemes coexist with new, and Ryumin is forced to juggle both. The mayor is trying to make Ryazan directly subject to the Russian Federation, thereby securing the city a place in the system of general funding and freeing Ryazan from dependency on an oppressive regional body. Meanwhile, although there is no legal framework for privatization or the materials to undertake the transition properly, he is trying to change the city over to a market economy. The region, however, is not anxious to give up its property, nor are businesses that break free from centralized ministries likely to accept municipal taxation.

Ryumin thinks that the period of transition to a market economy will require a decade, that its nature will be more Asiatic than European, and that it will depend on a firm hand and a semidictatorial regime. The voters themselves, he believes, will demand this. To confirm his last point, he cites the fact that four KGB officers have been elected deputies to the Ryazan council, proof that the electorate trusts the KGB and the army to stand up to local organized crime and keep order.

The mayor says he has "complete confidence" in Yeltsin, even though his team keeps making mistakes and Yeltsin himself, as a former regional Communist leader, is more in tune with regional than municipal matters. And in the end it is the cities that will safeguard reform in the face of rural conservatism.

In Ryumin's opinion Russia is putting the brakes on a military takeover. And Gorbachev? "I see no future for him," says the mayor firmly, "but I don't want him to retire, because I don't know who would replace him. Yeltsin can't, because the other republics won't accept him. Gorbachev will go down in history as the man who fought the system in spite of the Herculean obstacles he knew he would have to face. Have you any idea what difficulties he had to surmount in order to disconnect the nuclear button? Have you any idea of the strength, the courage, and the patience it required to do what Gorbachev has done? In October 1990 Gorbachev signed a decree to reduce drastically the number of generals, but he couldn't quite pull it off. As the decree went against their interests, the generals blocked it."

Ryumin is using all his soldier's energy to fight for a market economy. "Society cannot be expected to mature all by itself," he says. "It has to be made to mature, just as people have to be made to see that they can work in freedom. My job is to wake people up, to create the conditions that will make it possible for them to act."

The mayor believes that the first wave of reformers is exhausted and that the way must be paved for the next lot. "I can't possibly keep up this grinding pace for a whole five years. None of us can. I haven't had a vacation for two years. I can never get away from the city for more than three days. It's time for a new generation to take over, but it will be at least four or five years before it can do so, and those years will be very hard on us. My son is nineteen and at law school in Moscow. His ideas are completely different from mine. That's good."

Ryumin is a soldier; his son may become part of a new bourgeoisie.

Ryazan, 22 March 1991

13

———— ■ ————

Children of the Gulag

The city of Vorkuta, just north of the Arctic circle, has a population of 116,000 and is administratively dependent on the Republic of Komi, a part of the Russian Federation. Vorkuta is the urban center of the Pechora River coal basin, and was founded in 1931 as a link in the chain of Stalin's gulags. In these inhospitable hinterlands, tens of thousands of Polish war prisoners were interned, as well as Soviet soldiers suspected of treason (for having been unfortunate enough to be captured during World War II), citizens of the three Baltic states deported after their annexation by the Soviet Union, and German prisoners of war. The gulag's huts have been used as dwellings to the present day.

I F we were blacks, at least we could claim that our human rights were being violated," says Sergei, planting his feet on the frozen ground, which is as slippery as a skating rink.

In the dark, Sergei, Irina, and I cross the vacant lot between his home on Labor Street and the highway that links the neighborhood with central Vorkuta.

Labor Street is made up of rows of dilapidated huts, buried under layers of snow and coal, that slump awkwardly like tired bodies. It is an ordinary street in an ordinary neighborhood in a city built over decades by prisoners in Stalin's labor camps, gulag inmates whose bones are the real foundations of Vorkuta.

The ice creaks underfoot. It is the end of April, and the day's melting snow has acquired a shiny, threatening surface during the night. A raw wind blows as shadowy figures hurry toward their wooden huts, where they will still have to stoke up the coal fire if they want to prepare supper or keep warm for the night.

We cross a deserted avenue, named after a Russian poet, and one of the three railroad tracks that cut through the city linking mines, central heating plants, and freight depots. Alongside a foul-smelling sewer, I say good-bye to Irina, the secretary of the Vorkuta strike committee, and to Sergei, her coal-miner husband.

A taxi takes me into the city center. To find a taxi in Vorkuta is surprisingly easy now that fares have tripled and the miners' pockets, after an almost two-month strike, are empty. Across from the Hotel Vorkuta, a neon sign pleads for "more coal for the motherland" while another proclaims that "the people's welfare is the party's supreme aim." Meaning, of course, the Soviet Communist Party. Tomorrow these signs will disappear.

"The city council has decided to take down the stupid slogans from all over the city," Vorkuta councillor Georgy Kudrov has told me.

Georgy, who works in Yuzhnaya mine, is the leader of its strike committee. He loathes everything that smacks of "the building of socialism." He left the Autonomous Republic of Chuvash, on the Volga, to come here twenty-six years ago, and he is a born political activist. This is why, now that the miners have ended their strike, Georgy is already working out how to start it up again.

The miners are bitter at what they regard as a failure. They have gone back to work because their mines have passed into Russian jurisdiction, and they have thrown in their lot with Russia and Boris Yeltsin. Even so, they see no way out of their troubles.

Sergei and Irina have been in Vorkuta for eleven years. They came from Novokuznetsk, in the Kuzbas region of Siberia, with the intention of saving money and not staying here in the Arctic for very long. Seduced by the temptation of earning big money in the north, however, they fell into the same trap as all the other inhabitants of the area's makeshift shacks and huts. When the couple wanted to leave it was too late. Nor had they managed to earn or save all that much. Over the years, Sergei and Irina have been losing their roots, but they cannot go back to their native city, because it would mean having to evict from the home they left behind the relatives now living in it. Worst of all has been the horror of life in the far north, with its stark extremes.

Summer after summer, Sergei, Irina, and their two sons swell the throngs of couples with waxen-faced children who fill south-bound Aeroflot flights. Sergei and Irina want their boys to know about trees, fruit, and the southern sun. In the tundra of Vorkuta there are no trees. The most that this climate produces are a few stunted shrubs and the occasional birch, should anyone have taken the trouble to plant one.

In summer, the spoil heaps green over. My taxi driver, Tikhon Kasimovich, the son of "enemies of the people," grew up behind barbed wire. He remembers that the most wonderful experience in his childhood was seeing trees in Odessa when he visited the city, where his mother had lived before she was sent to the gulag at the age of eighteen. Until he saw his first grapevine, Tikhon thought that grapes grew on trees. He had got that idea from reading Aesop's fables and seeing the picture of the fox gazing up at the juicy grapes. "But they grow on bushes," said Tikhon, awakening from his childhood reverie.

When Irina and Sergei moved to Vorkuta from Novokuz-netsk, Sergei had to sign a paper agreeing not to ask his new boss for housing. So the couple simply squatted in an abandoned hut, without gas or running water, where they still live today. Sometimes they go to bed fully clothed, banking up the fire in the kitchen range before they turn in. In the morning, they throw on more coal. When they need a bath, they go to the public bathhouse. Their toilet is just outside the door of the hut. "Many women suffer from chronic cystitis," Irina remarks. All their water has to be fetched from a hydrant. In winter, at forty degrees below zero and in a blizzard, they take kettles of boiling water to thaw the pipe. Sometimes even after this dousing the hydrant may not work, and they have to walk miles to the next nearest pipe. The hut's board walls are lined with cardboard. When the wind comes up, the whole building moves about as if it were no more substantial than a shoebox.

A few years ago, Irina and a neighbor went to the party's Central Committee in Moscow to protest about living conditions in Vorkuta. As proof, they showed photographs of their respective homes. The official who dealt with them, one Vasily Vasilievich Vasiliev, handed the photographs back after barely a glance. "There are no huts in the Soviet Union," he told the women. But there are—any number of them. The Vorkuta huts are just one aspect of the hand-to-mouth existence that has been prevalent here for decades.

Vitaly Troshin, who is forty-four, is the city of Vorkuta's chief architect. A native of Leningrad, he left there eight years ago, and his face still lights up when he talks of how outspoken its intellectual circles were in the seventies. A circus performer before studying architecture, Troshin was on his way to becoming an internationally renowned acrobat. His act involved catching on his head a girl who came somersaulting through the air. One day in Novgorod a stroke of bad luck and a girl who was too heavy or too clumsy ruined him for the circus.

Troshin is enthusiastic about a big creative project. He wants to turn the city of Vorkuta into an enormous monument dedicated to the thousands upon thousands of victims sent to their graves in this desolate valley on the sixty-seventh parallel. Troshin wants to honor the memory of those who built the mines, the railroad, the highways, the brick houses, and the wooden huts that to this day—more than thirty years later and to the great shame of the city, the republic, and the nation—still house their descendants.

Troshin has observed that the city of Vorkuta and the mines that encircle it form the outlines of a skull, even down to its jaw and empty eye sockets. Everywhere, all over the landscape, are the recurring motifs of towers with their winding gear, spoil heaps, mounds of bulldozed earth, the black of the coal, and smoke pouring out of chimneys.

In the future, this skull will be the gulags' Way of the Cross. To Vitaly, co-president of Memorial—an anti-Stalinist organization, one of whose functions is to keep alive the record of the dictator's massive program of repression—the skull is a symbol of the deaths associated with Vorkuta. We are in a place contaminated, as Solzhenitsyn put it, by the "metastasis" of the gulag. The process began on the island of Solovki in 1928 and spread during the thirties. Ukhta, Pechora, Inta, and Vorkuta were sections of an immense chain of prison camps that embraced the whole region, the whole country.

The convicts traveled by rail as far as Archangel; from there they were taken by ship to the mouth of the Pechora. They continued up the Pechora and its tributary, the Usa, by riverboat, making the final stage of the journey, the twenty-five miles from Vorkuta to Kholmer-yu, on foot. There is still a mine in Kholmer-yu today, and it has gone on strike like all the rest.

Surrounded by cemeteries, Vorkuta and everything in it is a reminder of the gulags. Every factory, every mine came into the world under the watchful eyes of prison guards, and not much has changed in appearance. Some people still call the mines by their old numbers, and many miners work in conditions little different from those endured by prisoners in the gulags.

Troshin dreams of commissioning artist Ernst Neizvestny, who sculpted Nikita Khrushchev's memorial bust, to create a monument in local stone consisting of death masks. Ukrainians, Lithuanians, and people of other nationalities who suffered and died here will have areas designed for them by fellow countrymen. In Troshin's vision, Vorkuta, which has never had a chapel or a free priest, will have a church, the House of the Gods, dedicated to all religions.

On the right bank of the Vorkuta River, on the very spot where the city was founded, Troshin's plan calls for digging into the steep embankment a promenade in the shape of a huge cross. The inspiration for this derives from the wooden markers bearing the identity numbers of the gulag's dead. Some of these prisoners were shot, others died of hunger or illness, and still others perished trying to escape over the icy tundra. Four hundred mutinied prematurely when they learned that Stalin had died nearly fourteen hundred miles away in Moscow. Their markers remind us of that first strike, in mine Number 29. Over time, many of these thousands of crosses have subsided onto the snow or marshy ground. When lifted, they leave a clearly visible imprint of their shape. It is this image that Troshin wants to re-create on the riverbank.

His vision is of a Vorkuta that will be for the victims of Stalin what Mauthausen is for those of the Nazis, with well-marked maps and guided tours around the disused camps. Russia has always shown its dead more compassion than its living. This may be why the huts, which are reminders of the problems of the living, are such a nightmare to the city architect. When I suggested that Troshin and I go to visit Emilia Volotovskaya, a sports lottery official, in the hut where she lives, he was hesitant. "It would be better not to say I'm the city architect," he warned me nervously.

Troshin was afraid of being harangued and having furniture thrown at him. But Emilia turned out to be a long-suffering, kindly person. She had done her best to make a home out of a place that was buffeted by winter storms and whose walls ran with water in the spring thaw and split in the summer heat. Between the two climatic extremes, her wallpaper was ruined. All the huts are this way, like elderly invalids. There is no point in sealing the gutters, drying out the damp, or painting. Every year the problems simply recur.

In Ayachaga, another of the settlements that constitute the skull of Vorkuta, the style of the huts reveals that they were built by deported Germans. Again Troshin is reluctant to enter one of them. Instead, he takes out a piece of paper and a pencil and begins sketching furiously. He draws twin huts, set at an angle to each other, beside an open sewer that but for its stinking effluent might be a Swiss lake.

The pigs in a nearby pen grunt, dogs bark, and, on a brilliant spring morning, Troshin makes sketch after sketch in a frenzy of inspiration. What else can he do? Vorkuta, unlike other cities, has no restriction on its size. To house the two thousand worst-off families, Troshin calculates that the city council would have to concentrate exclusively on building homes. But that would still not be enough, for unless the vacated huts were pulled down at once new arrivals would immediately move into them.

In law, the huts present no problem. According to the city records they have long since been demolished. This is one reason why many young people from Vorkuta have difficulty obtaining internal passports. As their homes do not officially exist, neither do they. This is also why, even after nineteen years of endless struggle against rats and damp, Emilia Volotovskaya receives no help from the municipality. The creeping damp blackens her son's posters of Arnold Schwarzenegger and Sylvester Stallone. The boy left them behind when, having reached the age of eighteen and knowing no other home than this dank pen, he went away to do his military service.

By day Emilia's bathtub, with an oilcloth-covered board over it, serves as a kitchen table. The tub itself is illegal, since there is no drainage and the bathwater must empty into the yard. Emilia is lucky, for she occupies the middle dwelling of three made by partitioning the former barracks where gulag prisoners slept. Her neighbors at either end are more exposed to the elements.

In Vorkuta I receive lessons in prison architecture. The barracks, which gulag inmates occupied well into the 1950s, were first turned into rooms that opened onto a common passageway and later into three dwellings, each with its own door into the mud outside.

Rather than concerning himself with communal projects to solve the city's acute housing shortage and eliminate huts that should be condemned, Troshin is more interested in his pet artistic project and in special commissions. One of these is the apartment house that contains forty duplexes designed by a friend of his. According to Troshin, these are the first dwellings of their kind in the Soviet Union. He confesses that he finds strolling among the huts a depressing experience. It saps his spirit and kills all his notions about architecture as art.

Vorkuta, 26 April 1991

Epilogue

———■———

On How Some of the People
in This Book Went Their Own Way
in a Time of Great Historic Events

O N 19 August 1991, Major Vladimir Zolotukhin discovered
that old Petya, his father, had broached a bottle of his best
wine to celebrate the deposing of Gorbachev, whom he could
not stand. Zolotukhin was not amused. If there were to be a
return to Stalinism, Volodya saw nothing to celebrate. Not
knowing what else to do, he put on his working clothes and
began tiling the floor of his family home in Tashkent, where the
renovations started the year before were still under way.

That afternoon, leaders of the opposition group Birlik found
Zolotukhin laying tiles when they arrived to discuss the impli-
cations of the coup. They knew that repressive measures were
imminent. The dilemma the group faced was that of either a
heroic death or a tactical retreat in order to save the movement
for another day.

On the twentieth, Uzbekistan's Council of Ministers recognized the legality of the coup, and the president of the republic's
Committee of Constitutional Vigilance gave the assurance that
all had proceeded according to law. This was the signal for
settling accounts. That same day, Birlik's leaders were each fined
one thousand rubles, at which point, without a moment's delay,
they packed their bags and fled to the neighboring republic of
Kazakhstan, where they caught flights to Moscow. For the first
time Volodya thought seriously about emigrating.

On the twenty-third, the Uzbek authorities began to back-
pedal and thereafter quickly changed their colors. The Uzbek

Communist Party put itself out of existence by becoming the National Democratic Party of Uzbekistan. Everything changed its name and everything stayed the same.

Volodya Zolotukhin now lives with his family in the Moscow apartment he was given as a deputy to the Soviet Congress. But since the question of perestroika's capacity to be a springboard for army reform is no longer relevant, his position has become uncertain.

Zolotukhin fears a breakup of the Soviet Union, because the process would leave unprotected the Russians living in the republics around its borders as well as democratic minorities in authoritarian societies like that of Uzbekistan. Zolotukhin is sure that Islamization is bound to come to Uzbekistan, and he would like to see it kept from drifting into fundamentalism. "Islam as a force for promoting religious, cultural, and scientific traditions is one thing; Islam as a political ideology is another," he says. "The more democracy, the greater the safeguard that the state will not be founded on dogma. Conversely, the vacuum left by the Communist system is sure to be filled by obscurantism."

Georgy Khatsenkov, the former Communist apparatchik and founder of the Democratic Party of Russia in Yaroslavl, has been transformed into the epitome of the post-Communist businessman. A short while after our journey together, Georgy Fyodorovich resigned from the Democratic Party of Russia and joined the editorial board of a publishing house. His business interests were broad and ranged from the newspaper *Demokraticheskaya Rossia,* the organ of the Democratic Russia movement, to the magazine *Andrei,* a Soviet version of *Playboy* and the first publication for men to come out of glasnost.

One day in the autumn of 1991, Georgy Fyodorovich invited me to dine at his home. He had moved back into one of those good brick apartment blocks built by the Central Committee's special brigades. Roomy and comfortable, the place had belonged to a member of the Politburo. One of Khatsenkov's neighbors was President Boris Yeltsin.

Epilogue

Georgy Fyodorovich was now vice-president of Yakut House, a business enterprise selling gold and diamonds for the Republic of Yakut, in the far east of Siberia, which produced 90 percent of the Soviet Union's diamonds and half of its gold. Georgy Fyodorovich had a nose for making deals, and he bet on one of the elite national groups that had exchanged ideology for commerce. With considerable satisfaction and pride, Georgy Fyodorovich showed me around his apartment. We paused at some of the pieces of furniture, which he claimed were custom-built by the same cabinetmaker who made Gorbachev's furniture.

"I have more titles than a Spanish grandee," Khatsenkov said, ticking off his positions without going into much detail about what they entailed. Vice-president and director general of Yakut House, president of a firm of middlemen, president of the Russian Commercial Association, and so on.

As well as the diamonds and several gold-mining concessions, Khatsenkov also sold bear-hunting licenses. "We are ready to deliver whole, frozen bear to your doorstep," he claimed. I can personally attest to the fact that his statement was by no means preposterous. Dinner was well on its way when we were joined by a colleague of Khatsenkov's, just in from Yakutsk, who was carrying a bulky briefcase. Out of it he pulled a hunk of bear meat, which he handed to the lady of the house. Georgy Fyodorovich thanked him for the gift and invited him to drink a toast to the future of their partnership.

I could not resist asking Khatsenkov if he did not now find it unbelievable that he had once worked for the apparat of the Communist Party Central Committee.

"Unbelievable, no. Funny, yes," he exclaimed. Then Georgy Fyodorovich told me a secret. "The funniest thing of all is that I still eat in the Central Committee's canteen, just as I did when I worked for the Communist apparat. The canteen now belongs to the Russian government, and I get in on my Yakut cabinet minister's pass." And he added, "You know you can't get in anywhere in Russia nowadays without a special pass."

———■———

"Give me your honest opinion. Do you think Yegor Kuzmich was involved in the coup?" Rembert Paloson, head of the Kolomenskie Grivy sovkhoz asked me when we found ourselves alone for a moment in his four-wheel-drive car.

According to facts that had come to light since the attempted coup, it seemed unlikely that Yegor Ligachev had had anything to do with it. That is what I told Paloson.

He breathed a sigh of relief. His conservative views were a secret to no one, but he had managed to avoid involvement in the affair, unlike Vasily Starodubtsev, president of the Tula kolkhoz, who was the spokesman for Soviet agriculture in the junta that carried out the coup.

"Poor Vasily! I wonder who dragged him into that mess?" exclaimed Paloson. He had seen Starodubtsev in Moscow in June during a meeting to found the Peasants' Union, an organization of workers from the various kinds of collective farms. "I don't believe Starodubtsev was in the State Committee on the Extraordinary Situation for opportunistic reasons. He must have decided that drastic measures were needed to improve the economy."

I was in Paloson's domain for the first time. When I telephoned from Moscow to say I wanted to visit Kolomenskie Grivy, I was afraid he might suspect my motives. But I was wrong; he welcomed me like an old friend. It was a beautiful day, and here and there on both sides of the majestic Ob, against the softly undulating fields arrayed in all the tints of the Siberian autumn, daubs of dazzling emerald green leaves were still visible.

Rembert Elmarovich, the old warhorse of the socialist system, was in top form, even though the coup and its aftermath had been a bitter pill for him. Nor had he found it easy to get used to the disappearance of the Communist party, with which he had lifelong links. "I don't feel that the party is to blame. Why should ordinary Communists be held responsible for the mistakes of some of the party's leaders? People have differing moral values, but those with the highest were in the party," he insisted.

The party and the world it represented were still in full force on Paloson's sovkhoz, a model in miniature of a system that had fallen apart. Beside the sovkhoz's central building fluttered the red banner of the Soviet Union, not the tricolored flag of Russia. The statue of Lenin holding his cap aloft still stood among the Siberian birches. On Paloson's office desk rested the telephone directory of the party regional committee. It contained numbers he could no longer call, because the offices were empty, sealed up, awaiting whichever new occupants might arrive from the long lists of hopefuls.

A portrait of Lenin hung on the wall, and his complete works were in a glass-fronted case next to certificates of merit granted by a now unthinkable trio: the Central Committee of the Communist party, the Soviet cabinet, and the Soviet labor unions. In one corner were the flags and standards that Paloson's sovkhoz had won in so many socialist competitions.

Paloson had a single point in his favor. Thanks to his experience as a good manager and professional, he was able to feed people. He knew that the spirit of the times was against sovkhozy, but he was confident that Russian leaders would not dare to kill the goose that laid the golden egg until they found a replacement. Paloson was sure that common sense would prevail. He was therefore not opposed to change but only argued that it should come about gradually. "To break up the sovkhozy is the same as breaking up the Soviet Union," he said.

True to form, every morning at eight o'clock Paloson spoke to his farmworkers over the radio, telling them about things that were happening on the sovkhoz. Each day the name of whoever had worked the hardest the day before appeared on the sovkhoz's roll of honor.

On 19 August, Paloson was not immediately clear about what had taken place in Moscow. The explanation came during the night, when the local television station broadcast Yeltsin's appeal to the citizens of Russia. Later on, Paloson learned that a coded telegram had arrived in Tomsk asking for support for the State Committee on the Extraordinary Situation in the USSR. Nevertheless, the second secretary, in charge of the Tomsk Communist

Party in the first secretary's absence, made the decision not to send the telegram on to the district organizations.

Paloson thought that the brave decision to ignore the Central Committee's telegram saved many people, for had they received a party order they would have been obliged to comply with it. The order would have set up a conflict of loyalties that many, perhaps he himself, would have had difficulty resolving. Paloson had his own ideas about democracy and the priorities of the new era. He believed that the most important thing was to prevent the economy from slumping. As for democracy in Russia, "Here they talk a lot but do nothing. That's demagoguery, not democracy. Democracy needs orderly behavior and a strict sense of responsibility. What we have in Russia today is a parody of democracy." He thought Gorbachev was already history. Paloson supported Yeltsin, despite having certain reservations about him. Paloson was not ruling out the formation of a socialist or social democratic party or even a return of the Communist party.

Grasping my arm, Paloson took me to see his "pride" and his "shame." The pride turned out to be a luxurious Palace of Culture, its interior faced in marble, with a ballroom, a theater, an indoor basketball court, and sports facilities. His shame was the abandoned foundation of what was to have been a nursery school. The construction crew that should have been building it had gone off to a more profitable job. The pride, Paloson said, had been started before perestroika. The shame was a direct result of perestroika. Contracts made with the old administrative system had lapsed. To get the work done required a more realistic figure than the five million rubles Paloson had in the bank.

After the failure of the state coup, the government took measures to encourage farmworkers to get their produce to the markets. They were offered incentives more powerful than money. To this end, the government handed out vouchers that could be exchanged for imported goods. Paloson had been lucky enough to receive a little red Japanese vacuum cleaner. He did not know where to put it and would have preferred a tractor.

———■———

The farmer Mikhail Matsutsen continues to uphold independent farming in the depths of the province of Smolensk. He is president of the hamlet's branch of the Agrarian Party. Led by the farming writer Yury Chernichenko, the party was formed to represent the interests of Russia's new private farmers.

The farmers were overjoyed to receive thirty thousand rubles credit per head, part of the ten billion rubles that the Russian Federation had set aside to help private agriculture. With these loans they bought farm machinery, but as soon as they were able to pay the interest they found that it had risen to 15 percent.

Professor Nikolai Kharitonov is still teaching rural economy at Moscow University, but he no longer runs courses for would-be independent farmers. Over time, he has retreated into skepticism. He thinks that the Agrarian Party has not evolved sufficiently and that this is because it met with the enmity of the kolkhozy and sovkhozy. As a result, it has been impossible to organize an integrated farming industry.

Kharitonov estimates that the number of private farmers in Russia has increased; on 1 October 1991 they numbered more than thirty-two thousand, with a total of over forty-two million acres of land. Despite the removal of legal obstacles to private farming and the support of the new Russian constitution, Kharitonov admits to being more pessimistic than ever. "The general breakdown is getting worse and worse, and until there is any kind of stability it won't be easy to solve the problems of the countryside."

———■———

After the attempted coup of 19 August 1991, the face of Aleksandr Bir, coal miner and Russian deputy, went out around the world in what was to be the most unforgettable footage of the next three dramatic days. In it, Bir is recorded for posterity as one of the unsung heroes who stood beside Boris Yeltsin when he addressed the Russian people first from the top of a tank and then from the steps of the White House, seat of the Russian Parliament.

Bir arrived in Moscow on the morning of the nineteenth. He

had been in Poland studying local government with an eye to running for the office of mayor of Novokuznetsk. Fate was to decree otherwise. From the besieged White House, Aleksandr at once got on the phone back home to transmit bulletins issued by the leaders of the Russian Parliament, and he noted a certain similarity between his activities then and what he had done two years before, when he coordinated the Kuzbas strike. He contacted the workers' committee in Kuzbas and was assured that it would not support the State Committee. Things in Kuzbas were tense, and Aman Tuleev, president of the regional executive committee and Yeltsin's ex-rival in the Russian presidential elections, tried in vain—according to Bir—to drum up local support for the coup.

Bir also took part in the efforts of the Russian deputies to neutralize or win the support of the army. On a number of occasions he went out and spoke to the soldiers. He appeared at the Ostankino television transmitter; at Tushino airport, where two tank divisions of Central Asian troops reacted to him with total indifference; and at the Dzerzhinsky Academy of the Ministry of the Interior.

The decision to hold talks with the army was adopted at a meeting of representatives of Russian parliamentary groups held shortly after three o'clock on the afternoon of the nineteenth. Twenty-five people were present, among them the Commander in Chief, General Konstantin Kobets, and two of his aides.

Bir was in the White House at its most critical hour. We met there during the night of the nineteenth, and again the next night, when it was feared that the Parliament might be attacked by special KGB forces. At a meeting of deputies early on the morning of the twenty-first, Bir praised the "patriotic sacrifice" and resistance of those in the White House. As a memento of those nightly meetings, he has a Russian tricolor signed by all those present.

The reaction of the workers' movement was unequivocal, says Bir. By the twentieth, more than fifty companies in the Kuzbas region were on strike, and many others were ready to join them.

In Bir's view, the 1989 strikes and the failed coup have something in common. Both events gave ordinary people a chance to organize themselves to take action, a situation that the authorities had always dreaded.

"The authorities always believed in controlling the people, even though in fact people functioned on their own, organizing themselves," Bir says. "People had two faces, one public and docile, the other hidden. During the coup that hidden face and people's ability to organize themselves came out into the open. After the night of the nineteenth, there was no longer any need to worry. The people were controlling us, and not the other way around."

On the day of the attempted coup, Valery Ryumin, the mayor of Ryazan, had the impression of a repeat performance of his experience the previous September, when Ryazan's paratroops were mobilized and sent to Moscow. This time, however, it was no false alarm. At 5:00 A.M., an officer told him that the regiment had been put on alert and was on its way to Tushino airport in armored troop carriers.

Ryumin recalls those August days with all the detail of a logbook. At 6:00 A.M. on the nineteenth, he heard over the radio the first announcements from the plotters of the coup. At 8:00, he summoned the deputies and warned them that the consequences might be grave. At 9:30, after having evacuated all women from the city hall, he had loudspeakers set up in its windows. Using these, deputies in constant touch with Moscow kept the people of Ryazan informed about events in the White House.

Meanwhile, regional leaders—headed by the president of the regional soviet and regional committee of the Communist party, Leonid Khitrun—held a meeting with army representatives from the KGB and the Ministry of the Interior. Ryumin asked several municipal deputies to attend, but they were refused entry. On leaving the meeting, the head of the KGB announced that a local emergency committee had been set up and it intended to declare a state of emergency, during which deputies would no longer enjoy immunity.

Ryumin demanded an explanation, upon which the regional leaders paid him a visit at the city hall and asked him to submit to the authority of the local emergency committee and, further, to that of the State Committee, led by the Soviet Union's vice-president, Gennady Yanaev.

On Ryumin's table, along with Yeltsin's portrait, were piled the first few hundred copies of leaflets containing the Russian president's appeal to the citizens of the republic. Furious, the visitors threatened the mayor and demanded that he remove the loudspeakers from the windows. Ryumin replied in kind and threw them out of the council offices. The mayor then made his way to the regional television studios, where he asked for three minutes to read Yeltsin's appeal over the air. The president of the channel categorically refused. That night, Ryazan experienced a situation similar to the one in the White House. People gathered outside the council offices, and Ryumin and his men organized an armed guard.

"Twenty officers from the Ryazan Ministry of the Interior Academy accompanied the Russian vice-president, Aleksandr Rutskoi, and the head of the Russian government, Ivan Silaev, when they went to look for Gorbachev in the Crimea," says Ryumin. "Other academy officers helped arrest the perpetrators of the coup. The Ryazan paratroops that had been moved to Moscow went over to the Russian government's side under the command of Major Lebed and were permanently posted outside the White House in armored troop carriers."

With the collapse of the coup, Ryumin's adversaries fell like a house of cards. Leonid Khitrun was one of the first regional leaders fired by Yeltsin for having collaborated with the junta. With him fell the chief prosecutor of the province, and then the head of the television channel and the editor of the *Priokskaya pravda,* who had, respectively, broadcast and published the bulletins from the leaders of the coup.

In their places, the mayor appointed people he trusted. Freed from the tentacles of the regional soviet, Ryumin privatized Ryazan's three hotels, including the Hotel Moscow, and to test the market he sold four new apartment houses at public auction.

————■————

"Your party has just carried out a coup, Tanyusha. That's what's going on," Tamara Alaeva told Tatyana Merzlyakova when the latter phoned from Rezh on 19 August.

Tatyana was deeply offended. She and Tamara had been roommates during the Twenty-eighth Congress. Together they had warred against the conservatives in what was to be Soviet communism's last great gathering of intellectuals. Even so, the two women now found themselves ideologically far apart. At the time of the coup Tatyana had not yet left the party, while Tamara was among the leaders of the Republican party, a distinctly anti-Communist organization set up by the very first of the reformers to have split with the Communist party.

According to Tatyana, neither Tamara nor many other democrats had any idea of what the Russian provinces were like, nor did such people have to take responsibility for the provinces' very real problems. Tatyana phoned several friends on the nineteenth, including those she had got to know during the Twenty-eighth Congress. She phoned Yegor Yakovlev, editor of *Moscow News;* Igor Stroev, the Central Committee's secretary for agriculture; and me. What she found out, however, was not enough to make her risk everything on a single throw and change the edition about to be printed on *The Rezh News*'s ancient press. Things happen in slow motion in Rezh, and the issue scheduled to appear on Tuesday, 20 August, was already in press on the Friday before.

While other newspapers were making up alternative pages and holding them in readiness, Tatyana allowed herself no more than a small front-page, inch-long insert that began, "In view of Gorbachev's state of health, he is unable to carry out his duties as president of the Soviet Union." The notice reported the formation of a national committee under the leadership of vice-president Gennady Yanaev—and that was all. The rest of the paper was unchanged, and its front page even carried a newly out-of-date report on the Communist party's latest project. Entirely backward-looking, it was entitled "The Man Who Kept the Faith."

Yeltsin's appeal appeared in *The Rezh News* in its issue of the twenty-second, when everything was over. Two days later, the paper distanced itself from the Communist party by dropping the municipal party's name from the list of co-founders on its masthead.

I went to see Tatyana in Rezh in September, when the journey was at last possible. When I had tried to get there in the spring, entry into Rezh—a closed city—was still prohibited by the KGB. Tatyana had hoped until the last minute to be able to leave the party, and in fact did so on the twenty-second, one day before that organization's activities were banned. She said she had had a number of reasons for staying on in the party, among them the fact of living in a city like Rezh.

"I don't know which democrats deserve a monument, those who were in the White House or those who live in the provinces," she said. "None of you know what it's like to live in the provinces."

Tatyana was on the defensive. In Moscow, among people who thought as she did, she had felt free. In Rezh she felt alone. Here, the former leader of the municipal Communist party was still calling himself the "first secretary," as if nothing had changed. Here, members of the party committee went on meeting at the municipal offices as if they still had a job. Every morning, Tatyana saw them as they passed by the little wooden house where *The Rezh News* was edited and printed. Here in Rezh life went on as before.

Tatyana was the image of frustration. The things she might have done and had not! The things she might have been and was not! The whole province and its ugly city choked by the fumes of its nickel factory weighed her down. At home, every time she looked out of the window she was greeted from the facade of a building across the road by the slogan "Long live the heroic working class!"

Bread rationing had been introduced in Rezh, and the shops were even emptier than in Ekaterinburg (the new old name for the city of Sverdlovsk), the provincial capital. Still, Tatyana had a three-room apartment in Rezh and a garden where she grew potatoes for the winter. These were powerful reasons for staying put, for languishing in the tedium of true provincial life. Coming from Tatyana's mouth now, the word "provincial" had lost the freshness and innocence it seemed to have had before the coup.

Index

———————■———————